D1795109

AIRLAND BATTLE 2000

AIRLAND BATTLE
2000

Christy Campbell

HAMLYN

CONTENTS

Published by
Hamlyn Publishing, a division
of the Hamlyn Publishing Group Ltd,
Bridge House, Twickenham
Middlesex, England

This book was conceived, designed
and produced by
Campbell Rawkins Ltd
2 Barbon Close
London WC1N 3JX, England

Designed by Bob Gordon
Artwork by David Ashby
Picture research by The Research House
Production consultancy by Almac Ltd

Filmset by Tradespools Ltd
Reproduction by Anglia Reproductions

Printed and bound by Graficromo s.a., Spain

ISBN 0 600 50046 2

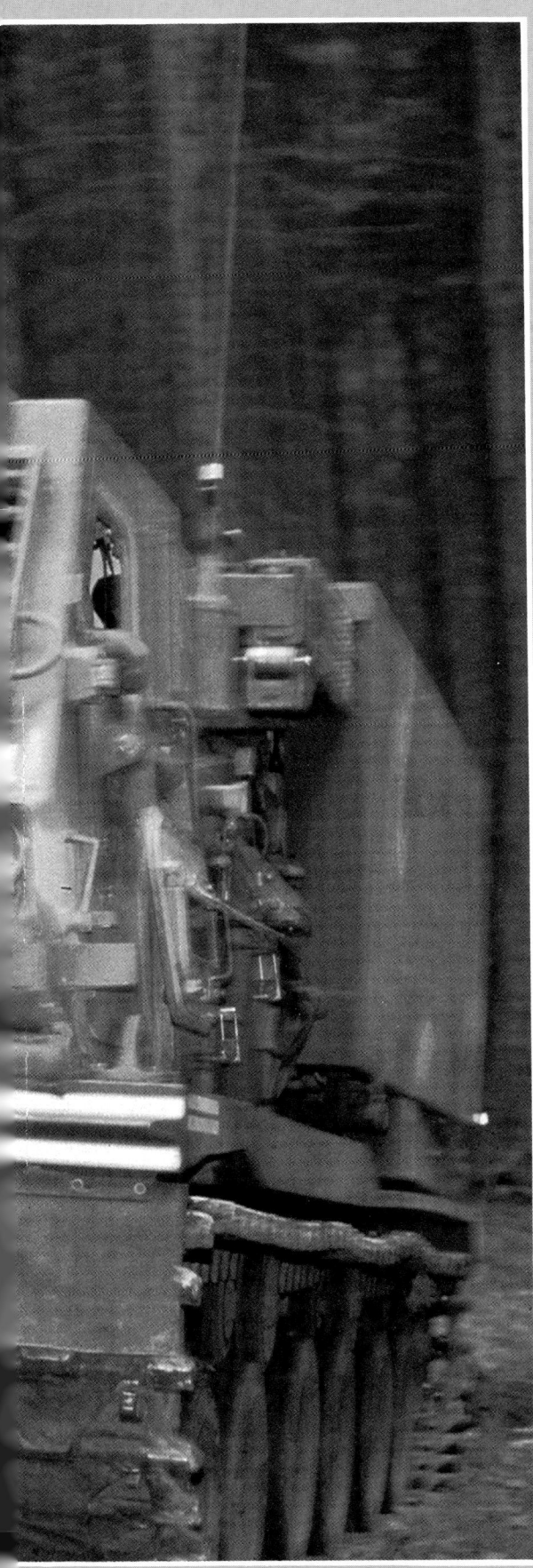

INTRODUCTION

'And we are here as on a darkling plain
Swept with confused alarms of struggle and flight
Where ignorant armies clash by night'

Matthew Arnold, *On Dover Beach*, 1864

All things military swim in an alphabet soup of acronyms. Surprisingly short and to the point is one that emerged in the early 1980s – 'ET', not a cuddly extraterrestrial visitor to southern California, but snappy shorthand for 'Emerging Technology'.

In fact it should be in the plural, a range of technologies that emerged from laboratories in the first half of the 1980s to become prototype production systems which are set to affect drastically the patterns of defence and deterrence for the rest of the century and beyond. The core technology of ET is computing – in military terms ET is all about harnessing the power of the microchip, and the lightweight miniaturised computing power it makes possible, to the battlefield, by making 'smart' weapons into 'brilliant' ones. A guided weapon like a short-range anti-tank missile has some kind of guidance system built into it by which its operator can keep positive control over it after launch. A 'smart' weapon goes one step further – after launch it uses the target as its source of guidance information, the target's heat for example, or its electromagnetic emissions or reflections. Such weapons have been around for several decades, configured for use against warships or aircraft which stand out starkly against the background of open sea or sky. Land warfare however presents a much tougher set of problems – many thousands of targets, tanks, trucks, guns and men moving upon the most radar baffling of surfaces, the earth itself.

Right: US Army armoured personnel carrier rumbles into action against a typical rural German background. Germany, NATO's Central Region, is densely populated and a key dilemma is how to plan a conventional defence, let alone a 'tactical' nuclear one, without destroying that which is being defended.

Below: NATO's Council in plenary session

Left: US Army M1 Abrams tank chews up the North German plain

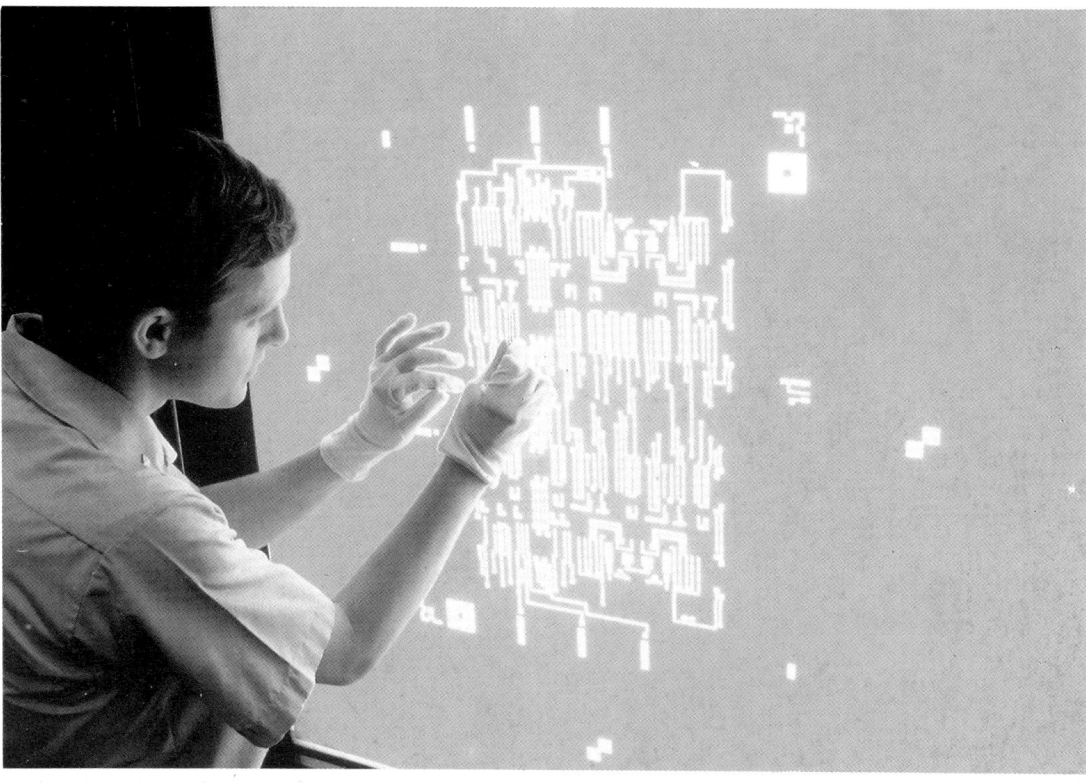

Right: A revolution in war or an evolution? How will emerging technology and the power of the microchip transform the land battlefield?

ET makes them vulnerable. ET potentially sweeps away the idea of war being fought at a recognisable front line. It blends land and air power to create the 'air land battlefield' stretching backwards and forwards in space and time, a massive envelope of potential destruction within which anything hostile, or indeed friendly, becomes vulnerable. It promises to make massive armed forces prisoners of their own size and clumsiness and thus is of enormous significance for the defence of the West confronting a potential enemy with immense conventional strike power.

Why there should be a conventional imbalance is a two-edged story embracing both why the Soviets and their allies should take comfort in massive land forces and why the Western alliance countries should feel secure at lower levels. The West has always sought solace in its perceived technological edge (driven almost entirely by the vast resources, competence and ambition of the US research and development establishment), yet one by one has seen its initiatives caught up by the Soviet opponent – strategic nuclear delivery systems, tactical nuclear weapons, penetrating strike aircraft, laser designation, electronic warfare and composite armour for tanks to mention just a few. Very rarely has Soviet weapon science set the pace by being first, equally rarely does it fail to match the lastest Western wonder device, if not with a certain defence then with an equivalent.

The latest Western initiative is ET. The hardware results of emerging technology are applicable across the spectrum of warfare but in particular it affects the shape of land warfare and thus the core confrontation of East and West in central Europe. What is new is the promise of being able to find and fix mobile land targets such as an armoured division on the move, deep within hostile territory and to launch weapons with a degree of autonomous self-guidance against them. Although such terminally-guided submunitions as they are called may not yet be said to 'think', they might certainly be described as holding opinions, such as whether that source of heat emissions down there is the hot engine decking of a tank or someone frying bacon.

ET is more than NATO's latest comfort blanket. It opens up a way of squaring the circle of forward defence and fighting outnumbered, the circumstances that brought tactical nuclear weapons to Europe in the first place and which prop up the continued political acceptability of the first use of nuclear weapons option. ET also sets a challenge to politicians and military policy makers, to use it to contribute to real security in this most dangerous of nuclear environments without it becoming just another arena for competition in the technology of mass destruction.

Military technology does not exist in a vacuum, nor does the policy which funds and nurtures military research, but sometimes they

Sikorsky UH-60 Black Hawk, the US Army's newest assault helicopter

do not march together. A capability may be delivered that goes far beyond that which was originally sought (offensive weapons in space as a result of defensive anti-missile research for example). The potential impact of ET on land warfare is at this stage of choice – using it to reduce dependence on tactical nuclear weapons or blending it into existing force structures and warfighting doctrines to make them even more destructively lethal.

Such choices began to bubble to the surface of alliance politics in the early 1980s. In 1982 the US Army adopted a new war fighting doctrine expressed in their key field manual FM 100-5, Operations, called 'AirLand Battle', which allied high technology target acquisition and command and control systems to a doctrine of offence to allow a 'deep battle' to be fought by land forces striking deep into the enemy's rear, if necessary using nuclear weapons if politically sanctioned to do so. Meanwhile the Supreme Allied Commander Europe (SACEUR) launched a political initiative for the NATO nations to adopt a new 'sub-concept of operations' called 'Follow On Forces Attack' (FOFA). This was presented as a much longer-term technological effort to raise the nuclear threshold by developing conventional but smart weapon systems able to 'strike deep' across Soviet and Warsaw Pact forces without actually using ground manoeuvre forces to do much more than hold the front line.

While FOFA and FM 100-5 were ringing in the politicians' ears, the US Army also published a discussion paper called AirLand Battle 2000 which set out to 'conceptualize' the shape of the land battlefield at the turn of the century, dominated by weird and wonderful robotic systems and bizarre military formations such as the 'electromagnetic close combat force'. The result was an immediate crossing of the confusion threshold which alliance spokesmen from SACEUR downwards have striven hard to unscramble, with mixed success.

Clarity is important because the deep strike business, however it is expressed, is everyone's business. Decisions already made and decisions yet to come will set the shape of the West's actual defences for decades to come, while 'Star Wars' inches its way through research at the edge of what is possible. Airland Battle is the official war fighting doctrine of the US Army and Follow On Forces Attack the officially sanctioned technological initiative of the Western alliance. Whether they work together, let alone whether they will work at all and do anything to reduce the risks of tactical nuclear war starting in the first place, is therefore a question of critical importance even before the intentions, capabilities and response of the perceived enemy are taken into account. This book tries to answer those questions.

'FIGHT OUT-NUMBERED & WIN' NATO's nuclear conundrum

'The people of this country have been so spoilt by ages of immunity from the actualities of warfare that they have literally no idea of the extremities of horror which the customs of war sanction, and to which great commanders have at all times considered it justifiable to resort to further the attainment of their designs'

The New Battle of Dorking by Lt Col F N Maude, 1900

A chapter in the US Army's now superceded FM 100-5 'How to Fight' manual issued in 1976 was called 'Fight Outnumbered and Win'. It sought to find an answer to the core problem in the defence of the West, how to resist an attack by an opponent superior at the conventional level without resort to nuclear weapons. Critics pounced on it as tacit admission of despair – that faced with a numerically superior enemy with a doctrine emphasising the primacy of the offensive, it was 'highly probable we will lose', and by that they meant lose the conventional war inviting the use of short range 'tactical' nuclear weapons in an attempt to hold the line.

Since the early 1950s, with complete continuity of purpose, the United States has offered up its own national destiny to the defence of western Europe against Soviet aggression by deploying both manpower and tactical nuclear weapons on European soil designed, not just to stop invaders in their tracks, but to 'couple' deterrence against attack on Europe to its own strategic arsenal. In this sense deterrence begins with an infantryman's rifle on the Inner German Border, marches through the Supreme Allied Commander Europe's own Nuclear Operations Plan, and ends in the multiple warhead ICBM silos of the American mid-west.

The North Atlantic Treaty Organisation reserves and still reserves the option of 'first use' of nuclear weapons as a deterrent against any form of attack. The consistent judgement of the Alliance's political and military leaders is that the imbalance of forces at a conventional level leaves no alternative to the possession of these short range nuclear weapons and retaining the option of using them first.

But is this believable? Would Western political leaders sanction the use of weapons which would destroy that which was being defended and begin what a former US Secretary of Defense called the 'cosmic roll of the dice'? The conclusion of many was that it was less and less believable, that the fact the Soviet Union had caught up on the level of strategic nuclear weapons and overtaken on theatre ones made 'first use' as a response to an overwhelming conventional attack an increasingly empty bluff. It was argued (it was an old argument but one that was always politically contentious) that the answer to NATO's nuclear conundrum lay in an enhanced *conventional* defence, but that now the West's technological edge opened up ways of redressing the balance without the militarisation of Western societies to politically unacceptable levels.

In the first half of the 1980s both the multinational North Atlantic Treaty Organisation and the US Army both embarked on technological and operational initiatives to find an answer to the conundrum. Allied Command Europe's 'Sub Concept of Operations' is called Follow On Forces Attack and the US Army's is called AirLand Battle. AirLand Battle is applicable to wherever the US Army should find itself called on to fight but its focus is firmly on Europe and the circumstances of meeting an attack from the massively armed forces of the Warsaw Pact. The two concepts differ in that FOFA does not include the precepts of deep manoeuvre battle by ground forces and is essentially non-nuclear but both envisage using new technology to be able to 'strike deep' across the enemy's forces.

To understand the Western Alliance's attempts to get off the nuclear hook it is necessary to see how it got on it in the first place and especially at how the forces and weaponry of the United States have affected that process.

The outcome of the Second World War made the USA the first global superpower, not just because of the atomic bomb but because they had developed the techniques and the strategic tools, the fleet and the aircraft to make war on, and defeat, any challenger anywhere, while forging an unbroken political consensus at home that this was an entirely appropriate thing for the United States to do.

Of the nations that fought the Second World War, US strength expressed as manpower mobilised was proportionately less in terms of overall size of population than for example the Soviet Union's 22 million or Germany's 17 million. The United States put 15 million men and women into uniform of whom some ten and a half million served in the US Army and Army Air Forces. General George C Marshall wrote in 1945 to explain why:

'It was because the US concentrated most heavily on aerial warfare, the production and movement of arms for its own troops and those of its Allies, and the meaning, in terms of manpower of waging war from 3000 to 7000 miles from our shores.'

Marshall's description of the nature of American military power remains true 40 years after VE day. Finding the appropriate allocations of effort between forces for long-range attack and troops on the ground, between manpower and the technological fix, between 'traditional' security interests and those nearer home, are problems at the heart of US defence policy making as much today as in May 1945 when four million troops were on the ground in Europe. The second great military fact of 1945, along with the perfection and military use of atomic weapons, was the presence in central Europe of the Red Army, the force which had engaged the main body of the German enemy for four years and ground it down to defeat on the Eastern Front.

Within a week of VE Day, Churchill was cabling President Truman: 'What will be the position in a year or two when the British and American armies have melted and the French have not been formed on any major scale . . . and when Russia may choose to keep 200–300 divisions on active service?'

The position was as Churchill predicted, by the spring of 1946, 85 per cent of the Americans had gone, 60 per cent of the British, the Canadians had completely pulled out while what

military strength the French and Dutch had managed to rebuild was distracted by colonial problems in South East Asia. Meanwhile there were 80 Soviet divisions west of the pre-war Russian border and powerful forces in Manchuria and North Korea, the result of the Soviet Union's lightning war with Japan in the last week of the Second World War.

For a while it seemed as if this mismatch of the military balance need not matter (remembering the fact of the United States atomic monopoly).

The Berlin airlift in which US airpower (with considerable British help) was used to bring off a non-violent solution to Europe's biggest post-war crisis

In those first two years of peace there was an assumption, however frail, that regional alliances and so-called balances of power had been the cause of war rather than its deterrent and what hope there was now lay in the United Nations to resolve conflicts and keep the nuclear genie in its bottle. That feeling was shared not only by the US administration but by the overwhelming majority of American public opinion.

It all unravelled remarkably quickly. In March 1947 the foreign ministers of France, Great Britain, the Soviet Union and the United States all met in Moscow to discuss the drafting of peace treaties with Germany and Austria – the talks broke down. Another effort held in London in November caused Soviet outrage when the US, British and French representatives agreed to admit West Germany to the European recovery programme as an economic and political unit. When in March 1948 Marshal Sokolovsky, the Soviet member of the Allied Control Council in Berlin, walked out, any prospect of remaking a single Germany was shattered.

More significant than Soviet intransigence was the shift in American attitude. In the spring of 1947, after British urging, President Truman went to Congress to request funds for the military assistance of Greece and Turkey against perceived threats of internal Communist subversion and external Soviet expansionism. Within two months, $400 million had been authorised. In June, General George Marshall, now Secretary of State, made his famous speech at Harvard which set in motion the 'Marshall Plan' for the economic rebuilding of Western Europe. Originally it did not exclude the extension of such aid to Eastern European countries. Moscow meanwhile saw it as an American plan to unite the bourgeois West on an anti-Soviet basis and to 'reinvigorate Western Germany's war potential', and compelled its satellites not to attend the Marshall Plan conference held in Paris in July, 1947.

The Marshall Plan was of course designed to do just that – to reinvigorate Western Europe's ability to defend itself militarily at a time when the Soviet Union was binding Eastern Europe to the Soviet political system. As well as those large chunks of the map which had been directly incorporated into the Soviet Union in 1945, between the end of the war and 1947 Communist parties won power in Yugoslavia, Albania, Bulgaria, Rumania, Hungary and Poland. In February 1948, Czechoslovakia fell in line after a Communist coup and on October 7, 1949 a Communist state was erected in the Soviet occupation zone of Germany after the year-long blockade of Berlin had ended any remaining hopes that Europe was not as firmly divided as the smashed capital of the Reich.

All this conspired to push the countries of Western Europe, if somewhat reluctantly, towards political and economic co-operation, expressed in such entities as the Council of Europe. The most significant immediate result however was military – the Anglo-French Dunkirk treaty of 1947 followed by the Brussels treaty of 1948 in which Britain, France, the Netherlands, Belgium and Luxemburg agreed to set up a common system of defence. Later in the year Field Marshal Bernard Montgomery became the first chairman of the 'Western Union Defence Organisation'.

Montgomery and his staff had no illusions that the Brussels Treaty powers in a military sense were virtually defenceless, certainly unable to mount a forward defence on a line of contact with Soviet power, dictated not by any geographical barriers but by the accidents of the German collapse, with only some 12 divisions and some 400 mainly piston-engined aircraft, in the face of the Red Army still mobilised on a war footing. The US military view of the time was that at least 85 divisions would be necessary to defend Western Europe from a Soviet attack, a third of them mobilised to hold the line of the Rhine and a further 15 to hold the Northern flank in Scandinavia and the Southern Italian flank. This was based on consistent estimates of the size of the threat as 175 divisions, but intelligence was insufficient to flesh in the actual fighting capacity of these divisions or the operational significance of the stationing of the bulk of them in the western military districts of the Soviet Union. Nevertheless the bogey of the Russian steamroller was as strong as it had ever been – and the feeling that the Western European nations alone could never match Soviet military power in conventional terms was paramount, as was the futility of attempting to do so. Security would have to come from elsewhere – from the United States in the first instance and beyond that from nuclear weapons.

But was the United States interested in defending Europe? The siege of Berlin accelerated developments. Not only did it mark the sundering of the wartime alliance but it brought an American military instrument, in the shape of strategic airlift carrying coal rather than atomic bombs, into the heart of Europe to bring about a diplomatic solution to the first major crisis of the Cold War. In June 1948 Senator Arthur Vandenburg's six-point resolution passed in the US Senate by a massive majority proposing US support for 'regional collective self security' – opening the way for America to join a Western European Coalition in peace time, not riding to the rescue as in 1917 or 1941–42 but committed to a regional alliance as a permanent component of world order. The American assertion of faith

Allied Command Europe: Organization

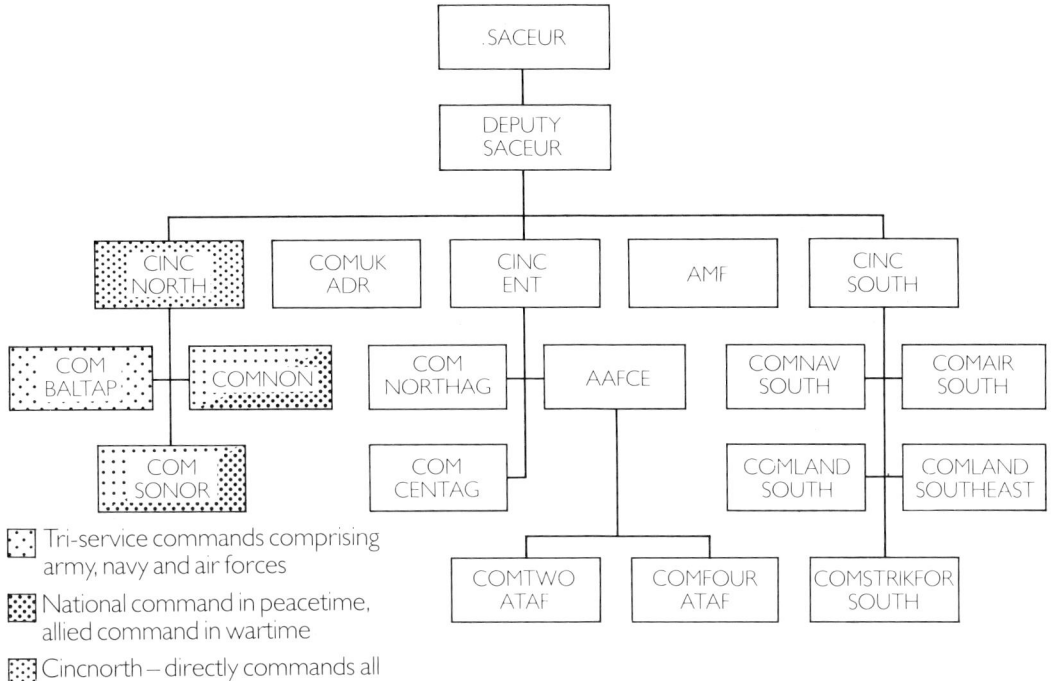

Tri-service commands comprising army, navy and air forces

National command in peacetime, allied command in wartime

Cincnorth – directly commands all the air defence forces

United States European Command: Organization

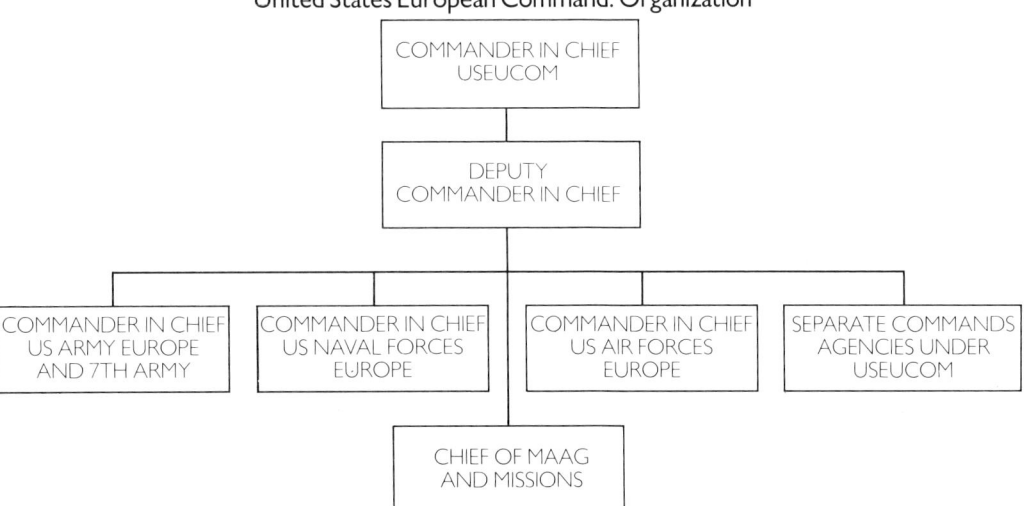

AAFCE – *Allied Air Forces, Central Europe*
AMF – *ACE Mobile Forces*
CINCENT – *C-in-C, Allied Forces, Central Europe*
CINCNORTH – *C-in-C, Allied Forces, Northern Europe*
CINCSOUTH – *C-in-C, Allied Forces, Southern Europe*
COMAIRSOUTH – *Commander, Allied Air Forces, Southern Europe*
COMBALTAP – *Commander, Allied Forces, Baltic Approaches*
COMCENTAG – *Commander, Central Army Group*
COMFOURATAF – *Commander, 4th Allied Tactical Air Force, Central Europe*
COMLANDSOUTH – *Commander, Allied Land Forces, Southern Europe*

COMLANDSOUTHEAST – *Commander, Allied Land Forces, South Eastern Europe*
COMNAVSOUTH – *Commander, Allied Naval Forces, Southern Europe*
COMNON – *Commander, Northern Norway*
COMNORTHAG – *Commander, Northern Army Group*
COMSONOR – *Commander, Southern Norway*
COMSTRIKFORSOUTH – *Commander, Naval Striking and Support Forces, Southern Europe*
COMTWOATAF – *Commander, 2nd Allied Tactical Air Force, Central Europe*
COMUKADR – *Commander, UK NATO Air Defence Region*
MAAG – *Military Assistance Advisory Group*

in the United Nations as an instrument of global security, like the wartime alliance, both expired in 1948, whose last two numerals George Orwell reversed for the title of his profoundly pessimistic view of humanity's future – a world in which all of continental Europe is absorbed by the Soviet Union into 'Eurasia' and Great Britain becomes 'Airstrip One' of the supra-Atlantic power called 'Oceania', both locked in a mutually self-supported system of perpetual military confrontation.

In July 1948 the serious work began in Washington of drafting a 'North Atlantic Treaty' between the USA, Canada and the five Brussels powers, but there was disagreement as to just how wide the new alliance's bounds should be set. Should Italy be included? Should the Algerian departments of France? Should Scandinavia be involved? And so on. Great Britain pressed the Republic of Ireland to join but the offer was declined. Norway agreed enthusiastically but negotiated a bilateral non-aggression treaty with the Soviet Union at the same time. Denmark accepted more reluctantly while Sweden clung to the neutrality it had successfully maintained through the war. Portugal and Iceland were offered membership because of the strategic positions they occupied or controlled in mid-Atlantic. Portugal had stayed neutral during the war but had granted the Allies airbase facilities in the Azores which had proved of vital importance in the battle against German U-boats. Thus in the end, the forming members of NATO who signed the North Atlantic Treaty on April 4, 1949 were Belgium, Canada, Denmark, France, Great Britain, Iceland, Italy, Luxemburg, the Netherlands, Norway, Portugal and the USA. Greece and Turkey joined in 1952, West Germany in 1955 and Spain in 1982.

The politicians who formed the North Atlantic Treaty saw it as very much a diplomatic statement that the United States would not sanction further expansion in Europe, bound by the promise contained in the most important of the Treaty's 14 articles, Article V which states, 'an armed attack upon one or more of them in Europe or North America shall be considered at attack against them all'. The soldiers tasked with setting up its military structure saw that any real deterrence would hinge on unified and strong defences in place, certainly more than the 14 divisions available when the North Atlantic Council held its first meeting in September 1949.

How should the United States best contribute to the defence of Europe? The great American war machine of 1945 had all but been taken to pieces. In the public perception, the possession of atomic weapons (the stockpile in 1947 was in fact a mere 13 weapons) seemed to override any need for the United States Air Force as a separate entity; Strategic Air Command was raised in status as the elite long-range arm of atomic warfare. Meanwhile the size of the US Army fell in 1948 to 700 000 men with only two divisions available for the reinforcement of the occupation forces in Germany and Japan. Although in 1948 Congress passed a selective service act to supplement the supply of volunteers with the draft it was only to operate for two years.

That earliest Alliance military planning of September 1949 did not, therefore, go much beyond plans for a division of labour in which the US would provide the means for 'aerial warfare' and seaborne logistics in line with Marshall's prescription, while Europe alone would find the poor bloody infantry.

Between the summer of 1949 and 1950, however, two developments occurred to make actual United States military commitment to Europe much more urgent than diplomatic promises. The first was the Soviet bomb test of August 1949 which broke the American monopoly, and the second was the outbreak of the Korean War in June 1950. Confronted with the Korean crisis, Congress activated eight National Guard divisions and then in June 1951 introduced a conscription act which ultimately made possible the drafting of three million men and the maintenance of twenty divisions in the field. Korea

The Korean War proved a bloody test of arms for US forces, 33,270 US soldiers died, 103,284 were wounded. Right: Heavy artillery in action Below: Mortars, the 'infantryman's own artillery'

had an important impact. It concentrated the North Atlantic Alliance on the prospect of meeting similar Soviet aggression in Europe, for which some suspected Korea was just a preliminary diversion, which would require a forward defence by troops (including Americans) in place, a major degree of re-armament and the establishment of a centralised military command under a supreme commander who, in European eyes, must be American.

Meanwhile the fact of the Soviet bomb made the Americans peer towards the horizon where their atomic monopoly would one day be matched. At the end of January 1950 President Truman tasked the Secretaries of State and Defense to 'undertake a re-examination of our objectives and our strategic plans in the light of the probable fission bomb capability and possible thermonuclear bomb capability of the Soviet Union'. The result, known as National Security Council memorandum-68 or NSC-68, was presented in April 1950. It was to be a field guide for the Cold War, couched in rhetoric that would be familiar thirty years later to get over its

message of unrelenting Soviet aggression and the military preparedness of the free world: 'We have no alternative but to increase our atomic armaments as rapidly as possible as other considerations make appropriate. In either case, it appears to be imperative to increase as rapidly as possible our general air, ground and sea strength and that of our allies to a point where we are militarily not so heavily dependent on atomic weapons.'

Thus in September 1950 President Truman announced substantial increases in the US forces to be stationed in Western Europe. There were doubters at home, unreconstructed isolationists who feared entanglements in foreign wars and the believers in all-conquering strategic airpower, but nevertheless the crucial decision was taken that American power would be committed again in strength on the ground in Europe even if just as a 'temporary' measure.

In December 1950, General Dwight D Eisenhower became the first Supreme Allied Commander Europe (SACEUR) and by the spring of 1951 he was presiding over a new military headquarters outside Paris with all existing US and British forces plus three French divisions assigned to his command.

The Korean War, however, demonstrated something else. Soviet aggression had been made in the face of the US atomic monopoly (the US stockpile stood at 450 in 1950) and yet atomic weapons could not be militarily 'useful' for the United Nations powers that fought in defence of the south, even if they were free from political restraint. Strategic targets in North Korea were just as vulnerable to conventional bombing while those further south, in China or the Soviet Far East, were politically proscribed. Tactical targets such as troop concentrations were too mobile to be targeted accurately and atomic weapons could not be used against troops in contact.

Korea also demonstrated how frustrating, bloody and expensive conventional warfare could be. The US Army was severely jolted in the opening stages of the conflict and urgently re-appraised its methods of training and discipline in the face of the near collapse of morale engendered by having to fight a fanatical Asiatic Communist opponent. Nevertheless the acceptance of the 'conventional strategy' led NATO rapidly to the doctrine of forward defence, and thence to the Lisbon force goals of February 1952. The targets agreed at Lisbon were very ambitious indeed – to boost NATO strength from 25 to 96 divisions within two years backed by 1600 aircraft, equivalent to the Allied assault forces mustered for D-Day, in the face of Soviet strength estimated at 140 divisions upwards.

Boeing B-47s, Strategic Air Command's first pure-jet bomber and the original means by which 'massive retaliation' might have been dealt out. Lack of range without multiple in-flight refuelling meant that they had to be forward based in Europe and North Africa to bring Soviet targets under threat. In-flight refuelling was used rather to keep a proportion of the force on constant airborne alert

The mighty Convair B-36, six contraprops turning and four turbojets burning gave Strategic Air Command a bomber with the range to strike the Soviet Union from bases in the US. By the early 1950s however it was woefully vulnerable to air defences

Nuclear Weapons come to Europe

The so-called 'Spaatz report' commissioned by General Hap Arnold soon after the end of the Second World War examined the atomic bomb's implications for the future of the air force. It reported not surprisingly that the precious stockpile should not be diverted from strategic targets and that overseas bases would be necessary to bring the perceived enemy within range – conceding that conventional forces might be necessary for the winning of such bases.

Strategic Air Command was invited into Europe at the height of the Korean crisis, establishing the 7th Air Division with its headquarters at South Ruislip, just west of London on March 20, 1951, and the 5th Air Division in French Morocco in June 1951.

These were strategic bases housing 4000-mile range B-29 bombers of the type that had dropped atomic bombs on Japan. That they were based in East Anglia or North Africa was coincidental to the fact that their target groups were within the Soviet Union. (The colossal intercontinental range, propeller-driven B-36 was taking a long time to get into full operational service and the first pure jet B-47 entered service in 1951. The prototype jet-powered B-52 first flew in April 1952. SAC began operations with mid-air refuelling which transformed the B-47 into an intercontinental bomber in July 1951.)

These forces would have been used in the 'defence of Europe' by making massive attacks on the Soviet heartland to 'stun the enemy into submission'. The revised 1949 edition of the first US strategic war plan which had been largely drawn up by the Air Force the year before, contained, on the Army's and Navy's insistence, reference to the 'retardation of the Soviet advances in Western Europe' as a specific objective of the plan.

The First Tactical Nuclear Weapons

Thus NATO's military structure was formally established against the background of the arrival of American atomic weapons in Europe and ambitious plans for large conventional forces. Technology, however, had not stood still, the research efforts of the nuclear and systems scientists were conducted with no less urgency during the Cold as during any hot war. Following the Soviet test, American production of fission bombs expanded rapidly. The possibility of building the 'super' or fusion bomb became a political as much as a technological option. Some ex-Manhattan Project scientists resisted the 'super', seeing it as an unprecedented instrument of mass slaughter rather than anything with a 'military' utility. Ironically they deployed as an argument an alternative strategy realisable through technology – making nuclear weapons even more compact with commensurately smaller 'yields', opening up the possibility of using them not as weapons of mass destruction against cities, but on the battlefield itself. In the end President Truman sanctioned both options, a tactical nuclear weapon programme was embarked upon and the first thermonuclear weapon was successfully tested on October 31, 1952, with a yield of 10·4 megatons, one hundred times greater than the explosion which destroyed Hiroshima.

The tactical nuclear option was of course attractive to those armed services who saw themselves as being relegated to the slow lane by the newly independent US Air Force. General Omar Bradley wrote in 1949 how an atomic weapon, 'in its tactical aspect may well contribute towards the stable equilibrium of forces since it tends to strengthen a defensive army' (to be fair Bradley was also a believer in large conventional forces). The commandant of the US Army Command and Staff College, Brigadier General Herbert

Right: The first nuclear artillery shell, the 15-kiloton yield Mk 19, first fired in a live test in 1953

Below: The outsize 280 mm 'Atomic Cannon' designed to fire it. It was double articulated and driven from both ends to be able to negotiate the narrow streets of German villages

Loper, directed that a manual should be drafted for the possible use of nuclear weapons in combat with the instructions, 'show me how to use this weapon tactically'.

In 1951 Project Vista was undertaken at the California Institute of Technology, funded by the Army, Navy and some Air Force money, which quickly and successfully demonstrated the feasibility of small battlefield nuclear weapons which could be packed into short-range delivery systems such as an artillery shell, or

free-fall bomb capable of being delivered by a tactical aircraft. The steps from feasibility to manufacture and deployment were achieved remarkably quickly, with fissionable material becoming available from the Savannah River and Hanford reactors in enough quantity to defuse the arguments of the long-range warriors of the US Air Force who still wanted atomic priority if not outright monopoly. In this they were joined by a vocal group of military planners within the most significant NATO partner – Great Britain. The Labour government of Clement Attlee, who had sanctioned the development of a British atomic weapon programme when the US Congress clamped down on international collaboration, did not share the American military belief in a nuclear solution for all military problems, urging restraint in Korea for example when President Truman hinted at nuclear uses. After the Soviet test, and the outbreak of war in Korea, they joined the Truman admin-

Right: A decade later artillery fired atomic projectiles had been packed into 155 calibre shells. This is an M109 self-propelled howitzer of the British Army

Below: Unguided rockets meanwhile gave a nuclear delivery capability at longer ranges. Development of the Honest John, shown here during a test launch at the White Sands Missile Range, began in 1950. 20,000 of these 35 km range weapons were manufactured

istration's drive for bigger conventional forces in spite of the burden of cost on Britain's creaking post-war economy.

When Winston Churchill returned to the Premiership in October 1952, he inherited the fission weapon programme two months short of its first successful test. Once appraised of the US fusion weapons programme, the Churchill government also resolved to pursue the 'super' but meanwhile the economic pressures of maintaining an imperial military commitment, the

burdens of targets of Lisbon force goals and rebuilding conventional armaments industries were proving unbearable.

Just a few months after reaching agreement at Lisbon, the British Chiefs of Staff sat down to draft a 'Global Strategy Paper' for Britain which reflected reality. They concluded there was no defence against atomic attack and emphasised the idea of the 'deterrent' counter-offensive. What was specially significant, however, was the abandoning of any hope of matching Soviet

US Army M109 howitzers tactically emplaced under camouflage netting ready to bring down nuclear or conventional fire support

conventional forces in Europe. What was required were small (and therefore presumably affordable) forces in place, capable of checking the Soviet Army in time for the atomic blitz aimed at its rear to stop it in its tracks.

Chief of the Air Staff, Air Marshal Sir John Slessor took Global Strategy to Washington in July 1952 and got a mixed reception. The airpower advocates lapped it up but the army faction of the Joint Chiefs led by Omar Bradley and others saw it as an excuse for a 'rationalisation of a British intent to renege on their NATO force commitment'. Meanwhile doctrinal ground was shifting in Washington, away from the conventional strategy as the crises in Korea and Europe seemed to fade. General Dwight D Eisenhower's Presidential campaign of 1952 had emphasised a balanced budget with defence cuts if necessary to achieve it. A basic planning document was approved by the then President Eisenhower in October 1953 called NSC 162/2 which laid out options for meeting the Soviet threat in the short and long term within the disciplines of financial restraint. For the short term it was deemed necessary to actually cut back on conventional ground forces while encouraging regional allies to shoulder the burden.

Behind them would be the threat and the promise of 'a strong military posture with emphasis on the capability for inflicting massive retaliatory damage by the offensive striking power'. This 'New Look' in defence thinking as it was proclaimed therefore raised the nuclear stakes, as far as European NATO was concerned, by pinning the deterrence of any form of attack to the prospect of 'massive retaliation' and by assuming that unwillingness to base more conventional forces overseas could be compensated for by tactical nuclear weapons. 'In the event of hostilities, the United States will consider nuclear weapons to be as available for use as other munitions' stated clause 366 of NSC 162/2 boldly. As a leading historian of nuclear strategy commented, 'The New Look uncoupled the response from the offending action. The West would not reply in kind to an Eastern invasion but raise the stakes of war. Thereafter Western strategy would depend on convincing the Soviet leaders that it had the nerve to do this. This problem would become progressively more difficult as the Soviet capabilities to fight at the new level increased.'

In the first three years of Eisenhower's first administration, total military manpower fell from 3·45 million to 2·84 million while the new Air Force grew by 20000 men, Strategic Air Command alone growing at 10000 plus per annum to reach over a quarter of a million in 1958.

The 'Special Atomic Demolition Munition', a man-portable nuclear landmine designed to wreck an autobahn junction or block a valley

But if the airpower people had the money and manpower to get their shiny new fleets of B-47s and B-52s into the air, how could the military planners at SHAPE turn the New Look into a doctrine for actually fighting on the battlefield using nuclear weapons with an exponential increase in destructive power unparalleled in military history? In early 1954 the then SACEUR General Alfred M Gruenther pushed through a high powered study on shifting NATO strategy to reliance on both long- and short-range nuclear weapons. It concluded that warfare in the future would inevitably be atomic, that armed forces rather than civilian population centres would be the first atomic targets, that the opening phases would be crucial and thus that forces in being before that early peak of destruction was reached would be vital to the outcome.

In August 1954 SHAPE recommended a major reorganisation scaling down the Lisbon targets with new, nuclear-orientated manpower ceilings. By the end of the year the North Atlantic Council had instructed NATO military commanders to plan for the first use of tactical nuclear weapons if the circumstances proved critical. Within three years these instructions to plan had turned into the formal adoption of document MC 70 which brought the Lisbon goals crashing down from 95 to 30 divisions and document MC 14/2 which enshrined first use at the outset of any conflict as the cornerstone of NATO's defence posture.

The US Army eagerly fell in line with the new thinking. By 1955, one half of the instruction and training at the Command and General Staff College related to 'special weapon' situations (that is tactical nuclear) and the following year the US Army Continental Army Command instructed the college to 'depict atomic warfare as the typical and to treat non-atomic warfare as modification of the typical'. By 1957 the regular course curriculum included 614 hours of battlefield nuclear weapons instructed per year.

The tools put into their hands in the mid-

1950s fell into three categories – so-called atomic demolition munitions (or nuclear landmines), artillery-fired atomic projectiles (AFAPs) and missiles with varying degrees of range and accuracy. Nuclear warheads were also developed in the 1950s for air defence missiles, both Army and Air Force controlled, air-to-air missiles and anti-submarine depth bombs. The first nuclear tube artillery system was the US Army's freakish and unwieldy 280 mm 'Atomic Cannon' firing the first AFAP, the Mk 19 developed at Los Alamos. This combination was used in a live firing test, Shot Graple on May 25, 1953 at the Nevada test site with a 15-kiloton explosion as the result. Thenceforward nuclear artillery shells were developed in progressively smaller calibres, 8-inch howitzers (203 mm) from 1956 and 155 mm from 1963, with ranges of up to 15 kilometres.

ADMs began to enter the inventory in 1954, land-portable versions of a free-fall tactical aircraft bomb, designed for the rapid creation of obstacles in the path of an invader.

Battlefield Support Missiles

The first generation battlefield support missile was the MGR-1 Honest John, a relatively crude short-range system with no onboard guidance, capable of carrying a 20-kiloton warhead over 35 kilometres. Other more sophisticated missiles followed including the short-lived Lacrosse and the extraordinary infantry-portable Davy Crockett which, even with a warhead weighing less than 50 pounds, could have a blast radius greater than its range. The largest Army system of the period was Corporal, operational from 1953 with a range of 138 kilometres and a warhead yield of up to 60 kilotons.

Having the weapons and manpower trained in their use was one thing – but would it work either in practice or as a cut price way of buying deterrence? The Army had not unhappily concluded by 1957 that atomic warfare might indeed by more manpower intensive, and not just because of its destructive power. Because they would be primary targets themselves for rival nuclear weapons, tactical nuclear weapons would have to be highly mobile, but would then themselves be vulnerable to conventional forces, requiring friendly conventional forces to screen them.

The longer range nuclear missile systems entering the arsenal such as Corporal also highlighted the problems of 'containing' any nuclear battlefield. Deep strike interdiction targets could be brought in range, providing a new 'theatre' component of nuclear targeting, blurring the distinction between the long-range attack and weapons for use on the battlefield only.

Through the late 1950s therefore there were increasing numbers of dissenting voices who doubted whether tactical nuclear weapons could buy defence on the cheap, whether the army's doctrines for treating them as very much more destructive versions of conventional munitions were appropriate, whether or not their use in defence would simply invite self destruction.

Two large scale exercises underlined the doubts. Operation Sage Brush held in Louisiana in 1955 was a war game in which a notional seventy tactical warheads were employed, all aimed at military targets. The umpires ruled that

'all life in the state had ceased to exist'. Exercise Carte Blanche held in West Germany the same year, envisaged 355 tactical weapons being employed by the defenders only. The results were 1·7 million West German dead and more than twice that figure wounded.

Nevertheless by the late 1950s NATO's ground forces, including the five divisions of the US 7th Army, were not considered capable of defeating the enemy. These forces were armed with tactical nuclear weapons to offset their supposed inadequacy compared with the Soviet and Warsaw Pact forces enough for strategic nuclear retaliation to be effected. (The Warsaw Pact is a multilateral military alliance between the Soviet Union and her European satellites. It was signed in Warsaw on May 14, 1955 as a nominal reply to West German re-armament.)

The US Army in Europe therefore had a strong symbolic purpose, not as a sign that American power would enter Europe once again on the ground to block a Soviet advance, but the threat of whose destruction would be the 'trip-wire' which could trigger the punishment to be dealt out by the long-range arsenal of Strategic Air Command.

Davy Crockett, jeep-mounted tactical nuclear weapon for the infantry squad. Its blast radius was almost as big as its range!

British artillerymen training with Lance, a dual capable surface-to-surface missile with a range of up to 120 km. Development began in 1962

From Massive Retaliation to Flexible Response

The successful placing in orbit of Sputnik 1 by the Soviet Union in 1957 was more of a shock to American feelings of security than the Soviet atomic bomb of 1949 or the thermonuclear bomb of 1953 had been. The huge rocket that put the satellite into orbit was relatively crude but it was technically capable of hitting the United States. The resulting 'missile gap' scare made the American people confront the prospect that one day their nuclear superiority would be overtaken. All this served to heighten European NATO fears that the doctrine of massive relatiation would soon no longer be credible. Not for the first time, but with increasing forcefulness, it was argued that an overriding NATO goal would be to *prevent* the use of strategic arsenals, in fact to find ways of capping nuclear escalation. The best way to do this, it was argued, was to go back to a conventional defensive posture. Others still advanced tactical nuclear weapons as the best deterrent, while seeking to make retaliation less than massive by offering a series of options on a scale of destruction. The Supreme Allied Commander Europe, General Lauris Norstad, made a speech in November 1957 which went a long way in arguing for increases in conventional capabilities and abandoning the trip-wire/massive retaliation context. Norstad argued that if NATO's frontier, the 'Critical line which 15 nations have vowed to defend', could be held with reasonable force then 'Force must be used to breach it. The decision to apply that force

would be terrible in its implications. The aggressor would consider not only the 'Shield' force in immediate defence but the sharp 'Sword' of our strategic retaliation.' The kind of defence Norstad was arguing for, while not diluting the fact that it could 'give pause to the Soviets *passing on the burden of further escalation to them*'. This was still a doctrine for tactical nuclear warfare however, Norstad making plain that 'The Shield forces cannot be considered as 'conventional' forces – for although they retain a conventional capability, their minimum size requires that they be equipped with the most modern weapons, including nuclear weapons deployed and available on a wide basis throughout the NATO forces.'

The strongest resistance to change in fact came from Strategic Air Command (in 1958 armed with over 3000 aircraft and about to form its first operational ICBM squadrons) who could not see why small scale aggression could not be deterred in the same way as large scale. Army Chief of Staff General Maxwell Taylor argued loudly for a strong capability in both tactical nuclear and non-nuclear warfare, but so frustrated was he that he resigned after conflict within the Joint Chiefs had broken out over a SHAPE-originated report which introduced the idea of 'deliberate escalation', a development of Norstad's 'pause' concept and a step towards the full blown doctrine of 'flexible response'. The Army lost even after the study had been to the Secretary of Defense and President Eisenhower himself.

Checkpoint Charlie, Berlin, symbol of divided Europe and of superpower confrontation along the border of the two Germanies. At the time of the Berlin and Cuba crises however, the United States in fact enjoyed massive nuclear superiority over the Soviet Union

Flexible Response

The 'deliberate escalation' plan was turned down but a new administration, with new people and new policies, was on its way to power. Senator John F Kennedy had long been alive to defence issues and had naturally leaned towards General Taylor and other critics of the Eisenhower years in his Presidential campaign. The new administration's first budget dramatically boosted spending on Polaris and Minuteman strategic missile programmes already in prototype form and strove to build a far more flexible range of options into the strategic attack plan for general war with the Soviet Union – the SIOP or Single Integrated Operations Plan.

While strategic nuclear policy was reassessed from top to bottom, the new Defense Secretary Robert S McNamara turned the spotlight as harshly on the European end of NATO's defence posture and the place of nuclear weapons within it. To the dismay of the Europeans, who had just got used to the 'New Look' and the budgetary advantages of maintaining small conventional forces under the American nuclear umbrella, the Americans were once again making noises about full scale conventional defence and even questioning the by now almost sacred tenet that it was 'impossible' to match Soviet conventional power.

The McNamara team set about analysing NATO versus Warsaw Pact military potential with the same kind of managerial, button down collar approach, wrapped up in the fashionable new science of 'systems analysis', as they applied to the force sizing of the US strategic deterrent – enough to 'wreck the Soviet Union as a viable society'. They examined basic economic and demographic data, levels of population, gross national product, technological competence, levels of output and so on and reached the almost heretical conclusion that it would be much harder for the Soviet Union than for NATO to support large conventional forces. The Pentagon team identified something called the 'PEMA paradox', (Procurement of Equipment and Missiles – Army) which put two simple equations side by side. For a total spending of $2·2 thousand million the US was equipping 22 divisions. Projecting that figure onto the Soviet Union's 175 divisions reached the astronomical

B-52 bomber, workhorse of USAF Strategic Air Command from the mid-1950s. This example is shown during tests for an unfulfilled proposal to re-engine the B-52 fleet with new technology turbofans

figure of $17·5 thousand million.

A detailed intelligence analysis looked at the combat readiness of Soviet divisions and concluded that half the total were below a basic index of firepower and counts of combat personnel. Comparing front line divisions' combat effectiveness with US equivalents brought a ratio in the US Army's favour while similar indexes were produced comparing tactical air power which were greatly in the USAF's favour, Soviet Frontal Aviation being judged a largely defensive force which could offer scant support of fast moving operations on the ground, if primitive Soviet logistics did not buckle first. What seemed to be a ten-to-one advantage in 1960 now seemed down to two-to-one – the conventional

option had never in fact been closed, the futility myth was exploded.

For the Soviet Army, the juggernaut of 1945, had not entirely stood still. Kruschev brought into play his versions of the 'New Look' with emphasis on nuclear firepower exemplified by the establishment of the strategic rocket troops and the introduction of tactical nuclear weapons and by a run down of the mass army. Soviet manpower strength in 1955 was 5·7 million. By December 1959 it was down to 3·26 million and divisions dropped from 175 to 136 before Brezhnev reversed the trend in 1960. Georgii Zhukov, the great wartime commander, as Minister of Defence from 1955–57 had striven mightily to modernise the Army. The corps was abolished

Right: Soviet infantry counterattack during the Battle of Kursk 1943. In the 'Great Patriotic War' the Soviet Army became the master of mass armoured warfare and even in the postwar nuclear age the tank remained the pivot of tactical thought. In the 1960s a new conventional build-up began

Below: T-62 tanks on manoeuvres in 1967

as an intermediate command between division and army and plans were made to retire cavalry and horse-drawn transport and replace traditional infantry rifle divisions with 'motor rifle' divisions. There would, it was planned, be two types of army division – tank and motor rifle which would be the building blocks for hard hitting tank and combined arms armies capable of sustaining conventional or tactical nuclear combat. Zhukov was dismissed in 1957 after noisy political clashes but his successor, Marshal Rodion Malinovsky, and commander of ground forces Marshal A A Grechko continued his organisational policies.

The motorisation of rifle divisions began in 1958. At the same time tank armies began to replace the cumbersome mechanised armies. The ground forces ceased to be an independent command in 1964 and were placed under the direct command of the Ministry of Defence but regained their old status in 1967 as part of the Brezhnev era conventional power build up.

The 'discovery' that the Soviet machine might be more than a little rusty suited the new men in Washington. They saw the uselessness of nuclear weapons in the kind of shooting counter-insurgency war that the 'containment of Communism' in South East Asia for example was

actually going to involve. With the Soviet Union beginning to challenge America in strength on a strategic level, it was also obvious that eventually the US nuclear guarantee to Europe would be compromised. Even if the target sets of Strategic Air Command were now primarily military (counterforce targeting) rather than cities, the Europeans could be allowed doubts that the Americans might not exchange 'Chicago for Hamburg' – and if the Western Europeans had doubts – then so would the Russians.

If the Soviets could be reasonably matched on the ground therefore, so be it, and the over-dependence on nuclear weapons could be blamed on European meanness.

In 1962 Defense Secretary McNamara reported to Congress, 'The events of last year have convinced us that the NATO forces in Europe must be greatly increased. While we will always be prepared to use our nuclear weapons when needed, we also want to have a choice other than doing nothing or deliberately initiating a general nuclear war.' But, at the same time Pentagon analysts who had first deflated the Soviet military colossus (Alain Entoven and Wayne Smith in a famous book called *How Much Is Enough*) also identified a 'despair and hopelessness' within NATO that had produced such weaknesses in NATO's conventional force posture – just 25 divisions with war supplies for a mere three days' fighting.

No wonder tactical nuclear weapons were so important. But were they still viable almost ten years after their introduction and after enormous effort had gone into building up a stockpile? The new analysis questioned their usefulness with some now familiar arguments:

War games tend to prove that tactical nuclear warfare favoured the side with more man-power, without reducing the importance of conventional forces to the eventual outcome.

– Tactical nuclear warfare would soon break out of a confined battlefield and would rapidly escalate into theatre nuclear warfare.

The vulnerability of forward-based systems near to the edge of the battlefield itself was an incentive to use the weapons before they were destroyed or captured by conventional means. It was accepted as Pentagon orthodoxy that nuclear weapons were something apart, separated by a 'firebreak' from conventional warfare. It might be possible to achieve traditional Clausewitzian political-military objectives through tactical nuclear warfare, but once begun, the uncertainties were great and the consequences of failure devastating.

The Americans had made up their minds

therefore to return to emphasising conventional options but they had to sell it hard to European NATO which was both reluctant to spend more on tactical aircraft, tanks, guns, boots, blankets and soldiers' pay packets *and* to see the American nuclear guarantee in Europe in any way diluted. President Kennedy worked hard through 1961 to urge conventional force improvements on the Europeans. The Germans were particularly concerned, Defence Minister Franz Josef Strauss pouring scorn on concepts such as the 'pause' idea and flexible response and loud objections were voiced to a detailed American request that the *Bundeswehr* should accelerate progress towards the twelve division army specified in the 1954 Treaty of Paris (in fact a target reached in 1965) and go beyond this to boost its force levels by six brigades at a cost of DM 30 000 million. Britain quietly ran down its manpower having ended conscription in 1957 in line with the Conservative government's radical Defence White Paper of that year which, like the 'New Look', had favoured nuclear firepower at the expense of manpower. France kept its own counsel.

At the NATO ministerial meeting of May 5, 1962 held in Athens, McNamara punched home the need for increased conventional forces citing the American lead as an example to be followed – a planned increase in US combat ready divisions

By the mid-1970s the Soviet Army's conventional force modernisation programme was in high gear. Vehicles like the BMP infantry fighting vehicle were unmatched in the West, able to transport a squad of infantry into the heart of the battlefield yet take on tanks itself with its wire-guided missiles and smooth-bore cannon

from 11 to 16 and the pre-positioning (POM-CUS) of material in Europe to equip two full reinforcing divisions. He offered help in the form of financial credit and equipment for the 'improvement in ground force strength and staying power' the Administration regarded as vital.

McNamara furthermore had a concept of flexible response which would impose further burdens on Europe. In his version any Soviet aggression could be challenged so effectively that the burden of decision to go nuclear would be placed on the aggressor.

NATO's declaratory policy was still MC 14/2 which called for a near-immediate nuclear response to Soviet aggression. In 1962, a new draft discussion document called 14/3 was circulated which revived the 'pause concepts' of the late 1950s. European NATO was as reluctant as ever to be weaned away from its nuclear addiction and the alliance governments dragged their heels. Political discussion was being diverted meanwhile by the 'Multilateral Force' discussions which attempted to set up a seaborne, ballistic missile-armed deterrent force under

Soviet paratrooper with AKMS assault rifle

NATO control, manned and paid for multi-nationally. By 1965 the MLF idea was dead and President de Gaulle was recasting France's role within the alliance. The break came in March 1966 when France withdrew from NATO's military organisation. From the beginning France had been most vocal in distrust of 'flexible response' and that distrust, and the pursuit of an independent nuclear capability, served to spread doubts in the rest of Europe about American nuclear guarantees. French withdrawal was paralleled by a new government in West Germany. Foreign Minister Willy Brandt and Defence Minister Gerhard Schroder were both eager to end continuing diplomatic tensions with America over German access to nuclear control sharing, and to open up a dialogue with the East in the process dubbed *Ostpolitik*. As the French fell out therefore the Germans came into line with flexible response. The British Labour government was broadly sympathetic although ever reluctant to increase the size of the British Army of the Rhine. Another significant development was the creation of the Nuclear Planning Group (NPG) at the end of 1966 which gave European alliance members at least a seat at the American high table of nuclear decision making. This further served to cut through the political suspicion surrounding flexible response.

Thus Military Council Document 14/3 dated January 16, 1968, and formally titled 'Overall Strategic Concept for Defence of the NATO Area' became declared alliance policy. It emphasised nuclear deterrence, forward defence and flexible response designed to meet aggression with an equal and opposite level of violence. But very significantly the Americans climbed down on the question of 'escalation dominance', giving NATO the option of first use.

By 1968 NATO's 28 combat-ready divisions on the central front actually outnumbered the Warsaw Pact in terms of manpower in divisions and in anti-tank weapons but this was still short of SACEUR's MC 70 target and the reserve structure was woefully inadequate compared with the Warsaw Pact's reinforcement capability. Europe therefore had only half been sold on flexible response. There remained over 7000 nuclear warheads, mines, anti-submarine systems, air defence missiles, free-fall bombs, warheads for ballistic missiles of intermediate- and short-range and artillery shells forward based in Europe stored at over 100 'special ammunition' sites.

The decade of nuclear plenty from 1952–62 had glutted Europe with nuclear weapons. The doctrine of flexible response might make seemingly more practical plans for their use but it offered no alternative to their possession.

Gradually therefore, from the formal adoption of flexible response as declaratory NATO policy onwards, tactical nuclear weapons became almost a matter for embarrassment within the alliance rather than for practical planning. Within the US Army itself, so called 'Prefix Five' personnel who had had specialised training in handling tactical nuclear weapons became fewer and fewer on the ground both as a result of the increasing involvement of the army in Viet Nam and the introduction of the Officer Personnel Management System which emphasised dual specialities. Rather than joining a nuclear elite, specialisation in the arcane mysteries of tactical nuclear weapons was a ticket to career obscurity.

As a leading defence analyst noted halfway through the 1970s, 'professional military officers tend today to be ambivalent on the matter. They usually are prepared in principle to use tactical nuclear weapons if the other side uses them first – or as something of an afterthought in case we find ourselves losing without them.' In 1974 however a new US Secretary of Defense, James A Schlesinger, came to office, a former professional civilian strategic analyst who proved anxious to find 'credible' options for the use of nuclear weapons across the spectrum – including the reviled tactical nukes. At the same time the emerging technologies of precision guidance had showed their potential impact on high intensity warfare. In the Middle East fighting of October 1973 it seemed, for the time being at least, that an infantryman armed with a cheap wire-guided missile might get the better of the tank. The last years of the air war in Viet Nam also pointed the way to the 'smart' solution with such devices as electro-optically- and laser-guided bombs being used operationally on a wide scale. The hope, expressed by Schlesinger amongst others, was that these weapons would raise the nuclear threshold by offering a 'gradual evolution towards increasing stress on the conventional components, a diminution of the threat of recourse to nuclear weapons'.

European NATO was suspicious but not as much as it had been during the flexible response debate. Issues came very much to a head however when the Schlesinger quest for tactical nuclear credibility met with a vocal technological lobby coming the other way, offering an apparent answer to the problem of using the short-range nuclear arsenal without blowing apart that which was being defended. This was the enhanced radiation weapon (dramatised in the press as the 'neutron bomb'), in fact an artillery shell or missile with a nuclear warhead which emphasised radiation over blast effects and thus seen as an anti-armour area weapon with the crews rather than the vehicles as the target. More than any other part of the new doctrine, the

Douglas Thor intermediate range ballistic missile. The nuclear tipped Thor, able to bring targets within the Soviet Union under threat, was operational under a 'dual-key' arrangement in Great Britain from 1960–64

MC 14/3 : NATO nuclear targeting

NATO's operational plans for the use of nuclear weapons are formulated by the Nuclear Activities Branch of SHAPE within the remit of MC 14/3 formally titled Overall Strategic Concept for the Defense of the NATO Area and revised in 1972 by a document entitled Concepts for the Role of Theatre Nuclear Strike Forces in ACE (Allied Command Europe). The basic nuclear targeting plan is the Nuclear Operations Plan (NOP) of SACEUR designed for 'the execution of nuclear strikes with the theatre nuclear weapons under his command'. These breakdown as –

Tactical Nuclear Weapons
2250 artillery shells
1850 free fall bombs
700 Nike Hercules SAMs (to be replaced by non nuclear Patriot)
400 ASW weapons
300 atomic demolition munitions (nuclear land mines)
72 Pershing la (German air force)
90 Honest John (Greece, Turkey)
97 Lance (36 US, 61 with UK, Belgium, RG, Italy, Netherlands)

British Army Lance missile blasts off from its launcher. Nuclear warheads are kept in US custody

Tomahawk ground-launched cruise missile battery deployed in woods. The system's mobility is supposed to ensure its survival should war in Europe escalate to 'theatre nuclear' level

Theatre systems

Nuclear capable aircraft include ground attack Tornados, F-16s, F-4s, Jaguars and F-111s. The advanced Harrier AV-8B which will enter Royal Air Force and US Marine Corps service in 1986 will be nuclear capable. Carrier based aircraft include US Navy A-6s, F-4Ks and Royal Navy Sea Harriers. French Navy carrier based Super Etendards and Armée de l'Air Mirage 2000Ns are also nuclear capable but outside the NOP.

The target for the theatre nuclear force modernis-ation process agreed by NATO in 1979 and commenced operationally at the end of 1983 is 108 Pershing II (all based in West Germany), 464 Tomahawk GLCM (96 FRG, 112 Italy, 48 Belgium, 48 Netherlands, 160 UK). The SIOP also allots 400 Poseidon warheads to SACEUR's target list. France deploys 42 Pluton short range missiles (to be replaced by a longer range system called Hades) and some 110 nuclear capable aircraft including carrier aircraft. French systems are not included in SACEUR's Nuclear Operations Plan.

MC 14/3 differentiates between three kinds of nuclear response – direct retaliation, deliberate escalation by selective use and general nuclear response. The current planning for 'selective use' involves the release of 'packages' of weapons defined as a 'group of nuclear weapons of specified yields for employment in a specified area within a limited time frame to support a tactical contingency'. Such packages could be a small number of long range weapons to a 'corps package' of more than a hundred short range weapons.

General nuclear response would involve the launching of NATO's long range system such as GLCMs and Pershing II at targets deep in Warsaw Pact rear areas and, significantly would only be invoked as part of the SIOP, the US central strategic war plan. The type of targets known to be included in the NOP include airfields, communications targets such as railway marshalling yards, Soviet nuclear delivery systems such as medium range ballistic missiles, underground command bunkers, SAM sites, tank concentrations, troop concentrations, ammunition, weapon and fuel dumps, lines of communication, bridges, harbours etc.

Pershing II operated in Europe by the US Army. A ground mapping terminal guidance radar in the nose makes the missile highly accurate while from launch in West Germany it could reach targets in the Soviet Union in under ten minutes

Royal artillery gunners with the nuclear capable M110 8-inch self-propelled howitzer. The M422 round has a yield of up to 2 kilotons

FE 14

Two events in 1979 combined to worsen superpower relationships, the Soviet invasion of Afghanistan (guerillas with a captured Soviet armoured car, right) and NATO's own Theatre Nuclear Force modernisation decision. Below: US airmen prepare to defend a cruise missile launch site

neutron bomb debate polarised political forces within NATO around the question of how far should one make nuclear 'war-fighting' more practicable, weighing any increased credibility in battlefield use with the prospect of stumbling towards all-out nuclear war.

This was not all. The spotlight also fell on those longer range systems earmarked for rear echelon attacks and deep interdiction – the so-called theatre nuclear forces such as F-111 fighter bombers or Pershing 1a IRBMs which were also gently marching towards obsolescence. Soviet modernisation priorities meanwhile were targeted just at this kind of weapon with mass deployment of the SS-20 intermediate range ballistic missile with a triple MIRV warhead

proceeding apace from 1976 onwards. The West German government was particularly vocal on the threat of the SS-20s and advanced within NATO the notion of matching the new threat with a 'Euro-strategic' response, that is matching the Soviet weapons with US equivalents forward based in Europe to couple the nuclear defence of Europe to the core US strategic arsenal.

In December 1979 the NATO governments agreed to deploy a mix of US medium-range ballistic missiles (108 Pershing IIs) and cruise (484 ground-launched cruise missiles) (GLCMs) with bases in several European countries. The thrust of the decision was to re-establish the theatre level in the spectrum of flexible response without uncoupling the defence of Europe from

the use of US strategic forces, although many argued the opposite was true – that deployment of such accurate and short flight time systems (in the case of the Pershing IIs) would allow the US to 'fight' a nuclear war with the Soviet Union from European soil. Thus, although American owned and manned and under US operational control, it was decided the new missiles should be land based to emphasise political visibility and there should be enough of them to make a difference but without making the fears of the 'war-fighters' too believable.

In the last years of the 1970s therefore the neutron bomb and theatre nuclear force modernisation controversies brought defence issues to the forefront of the political agenda in European NATO countries where they have remained ever since, much more effectively in fact than the continued Soviet deployment of new-generation theatre nuclear forces and conventional force modernisation. It was especially ironic perhaps that in the decade in which conventional weapons showed themselves capable of exponential increases in firepower, NATO's nuclear conundrums would be heightened as never before.

STRIKE DEEP: The conventional option

'NATO's lack of consistent resolve in providing a credible conventional capability has led to our having mortgaged our defense to nuclear response'

General Bernard Rogers, Supreme Allied Commander Europe, 1982

The agreement by NATO governments of a long term *conventional* improvement programme in May 1978 was achieved with only a fraction of the political alarms and excursions that would accompany the nuclear initiatives. There had been a tremendous scare in the mid-1970s that Warsaw Pact forces could overwhelm NATO's forces very quickly and effectively with just 29 divisions, without the long and presumably detectable mobilisation period which had been built into previous defensive plans in which enemy strength would peak only 30 days following mobilisation. The new 'scenario' reduced political warning time to zero with the enemy coming into action a few hours after leaving their assembly areas and crossing the Rhine within 48 hours.

This alarmist stuff was subsequently played down but it stiffened the political sinews for NATO defence ministers to get through the Long Term Defence Programme (LTDP) agreed at the May 1978 NATO summit and the concurrent decision to generate annual defence budget increases of three per cent in real terms across five years from 1979 onwards. Quick fix improvements were essentially complete by 1979 especially in war reserve ammunition and anti-tank weapons. Stocks of air-to-air, ground-to-ground and anti-tank missiles were increased while the armour imbalance problem was addressed by increasing heavy anti-tank guided missile deployments such as TOWs on helicopters while the latest electro-optical and laser ranging and target designation devices were given priority. The LTDP formally identified ten key areas for special attention: theatre nuclear force modernisation; readiness, aimed at improving the alert times of standing forces, reserve units and civil support; air defence; maritime improvement programme; command, control and communications; electronic warfare; reinforcement programme; reserve mobilisation; consumer logistics; and rationalisation, that is the search for standardisation and compatability of systems which is now a traditional if as yet incompletely attained NATO goal.

Right: Israeli TOW anti-tank gunners. During the Yom Kippur war of 1973 the stopping power of the wire-guided anti-tank missiles gave the military doctrine writers of the world cause for thought. The US Army made great play of this 'new lethality' in its 'Active Defense' doctrine of the mid-1970s

Left: Swedish infantry armed with wire-guided anti-tank missiles. The Swedes, like the armies of other neutral nations are tied to a policy of territorial defence. They seek to deter the invader with the prospect of tangling with a whole nation in arms

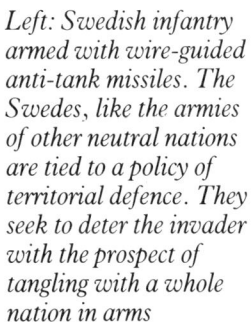

The Doctrinal Dilemmas of Defence

The urgency of the long-term improvement programme and the agreement to spend more on defence against a background of economic recession in the industrialised West emphasised NATO's new seriousness about conventional defence. The tactical nuclear solution of the '50s and '60s had pushed into the background the strategic dilemmas which had always attended the Alliance's conventional defence posture. It has always been complicated by the prescription of forward defence, of not trading ground, a doctrine driven by German unwillingness to cede national territory or indeed have a 'limited' nuclear war fought on German soil. Originally iʳ was a political expedient but once France left NATO's political command structure in 1967, forward defence became a military necessity because of the closeness of critical North Sea supply ports to any point of breakthrough and the simple geographical narrowness of West Germany, the border with the East dictated not by any natural barrier but by the accidents of the 1945 armistice. The second great dilemma of the West's defence is that, compared with the force structure of the Soviet Union and Warsaw Pact, the most powerful member of the Western alliance is physically separated from the area of contention by the Atlantic Ocean. Third is that the Soviet Union provides a far greater proportion of Warsaw Pact combat power and standardised equipment than does the US for NATO in Europe (the US provides ten per cent of NATO's ground forces, 20 per cent of its seapower, and 25 per cent of its tactical airpower).

The burden of NATO's conventional military planning, therefore, has long been how to contain an offensive by a numerically superior opponent and do it without trading ground, long enough for US, Canadian and British reinforcements to be mobilised and safely delivered to hold the line in Europe before as the first tactical nuclear weapons went off.

How to do it? NATO had always comforted itself in a perceived qualitative advantage in its weapons technology. The US Army's operational Field Manual of the 1970s prescribed the doctrine of Active Defence in which the 'new lethality' of modern weapon systems supposedly gave the defence the upper hand. Through the last years of the decade, confidence in this comfortable assumption was being chipped away, both by doubters within the military establishment and the fact that Soviet technology was catching up on the conventional level.

The US Army maintains stores of so-called 'POMCUS' equipment (Prepositioning of Material Configured to Unit Sets) forward based in Europe awaiting the arrival of reinforcement manpower

US infantryman firing Dragon, the US Army's standard man-portable anti-tank weapon since 1975. The operator is told to hold his breath during the missile's 12-second flight time and 'not to blink when the motor fires'

But the Soviets were only catching up with what NATO already had in place. NATO's qualitative edge was alive and well but inside the research and development (R & D) programmes of the US Air Force, US Army and the Defense Advanced Projects Agency (DARPA) which had been pumping out R & D money into industry and academia since the end of the Viet Nam war. The microchip was set not just to change the industrial and social patterns of the West – it was set to transform the technology of the battlefield, the place where that social system constantly tested itself in perpetual military confrontation with its ideological enemy. This was the situation which set to make the export of a home computer to a Communist bloc country become a treasonable act. 'Emerging Technology' (ET) was the key although NATO officials are at pains to point out that it is not a magic wand. The rate of technological change is 'evolutionary' rather than revolutionary so they say, with no 'Buck Rodgers' weaponry.

Although improvements in conventional weapons technology was not accorded a separate task force as theatre nuclear weapons had been in the Long Term Defence Programme, it was regarded as the implicit common denominator. In 1982 the US Secretary of Defense Caspar Weinberger repeatedly pressed on NATO defence ministers the idea of harnessing the power of emerging technologies to conventional defence. In his FY 1984 report to Congress Weinberger reported 'At the NATO Defense Ministers meeting in May 1982, I proposed that the Alliance undertake an immediate study on exploiting new technologies for the improvement of our conventional defense. At the December 1982 Ministerial meeting, I presented the US proposal for initiating this NATO-wide effort for improving conventional defense in the primary areas of defense against first echelon attack, interdiction of Warsaw Pact follow-on forces, improving counter-air capability, enhancing command, control and communications and intelligence capabilities and disrupting Warsaw Pact C^3.'

NATO was already more than warmed up for the Weinberger initiative. One of General Bernard W Rogers' first actions on being appointed Supreme Allied Commander Europe (SACEUR) in 1979 was to put in hand an intensive study of Allied Command Europe's conventional strength and its ability to meet the precepts of both flexible response and forward defence before resort to nuclear weapons. SACEUR was not comforted by the result.

Analysis of NATO's own shortcomings turned to those of the opposition. The Soviet Army with its Warsaw Pact satellites was a massive opponent but there was only so much

room for them to pile up enough strength on NATO's Central Region to be confident of the very rapid breakthrough they prized – hence the Soviet doctrine of attacking in successively staged 'echelons' with so-called 'follow on forces' arrayed so as to punch a hole in a defence with successive blows. As the first echelon burnt itself out, the second would arrive to break through the equally battered defenders. The Soviets had depth in their doctrine of the offensive. NATO with forward defence did not. The only acceptable way to add depth to the defence was to attack the follow-on forces before they arrived at the main battle area, at the so-called Forward Edge of the Battle Area or FEBA. The 'discovery' of the opponent's principle of echeloning was the key, the original work concentrating on improving the existing means for battlefield interdiction such as manned aircraft both to attack mobile second echelon forces, and their communications and logistics. After the second 'discovery' of the Soviet Operational Manoeuvre Group (see Chapter 5) the SHAPE team began to refer to all forces behind the troops in actual contact as 'follow on forces'. After two years of intensive work, the 'ACE FOFA' (Allied Command Europe Follow On Formation Attack) 'Subconcept of Operations' was completed in mid-June, 1981.

Left: General Bernard Rogers, Supreme Allied Commander Europe (SACEUR) since 1979 and moving spirit behind the Follow on Forces Attack concept

Right: US Army M60A1 tank rumbles into action on manoeuvres in Germany

Below: Troops of the British Army of the Rhine race to a pick-up by Chinook helicopter during Operation Lionheart, large scale manoeuvres conducted in 1984

After a personal presentation by SACEUR the idea was approved by NATO's Military Committee in October 1981. General Rogers set out with a will to sell it to the politicians who would have to formally agree to adoption of the doctrine as Alliance policy and find the money to procure the advanced weapon systems that it would require. Throughout 1982 SACEUR hammered home the message, using the first use tactical nuclear conundrum to gain attention and support against the already highly volatile background of alliance politics created by the theatre nuclear force modernisation decision. In an influential speech delivered in London in September 1982 SACEUR put it at its most succinct – 'NATO's lack of consistent resolve in providing a credible conventional capability has led to our having mortgaged our defense to the nuclear response'.

General Rogers held no brief for those who would abandon first use on moral grounds but he went on to say, 'we do need a conventional capability adequate enough to provide a reasonable prospect of success using NATO's preferred response, to defeat an attack or place the burden of escalation on the attacker', in effect forcing them to go nuclear first. This was a very appetising political bait. In March of 1982 the

NATO defence ministers got the FOFA message. In the summer it was the turn of the three and four star generals at the Shapex '82 conference. By autumn the Defence Planning Committee had agreed force goals for the period 1983–88 based on SACEUR's own force proposals for ACE FOFA and were considering a Long Term Planning Guideline (LTPG) for the proposal, formal approval of which would be a requisite step before the means to implement FOFA could be formally analysed and agreement reached on how to provide those means. On 9 November, 1984 SACEUR's long term planning guideline for follow on formation attack was formally agreed by the Defense Planning Committee after eighteen months of briskly argued internal debate. The issues at stake were taken up robustly by specialist defence commentators in the media but barely caused a ripple in the wider political consciousness of the Alliance nations, compared that is with the anguish which followed the TNF modernisation decision of December 1979.

But arguments there were. They hinged on the relative apportion of effort between defence at the front line and attacking the follow on formations. Whether the equipping and mobilisation of reserve manpower was a better option

Soviet Military Echelons

A simplified diagram of how the West's military analysts perceive the Soviet principle of 'echeloning'

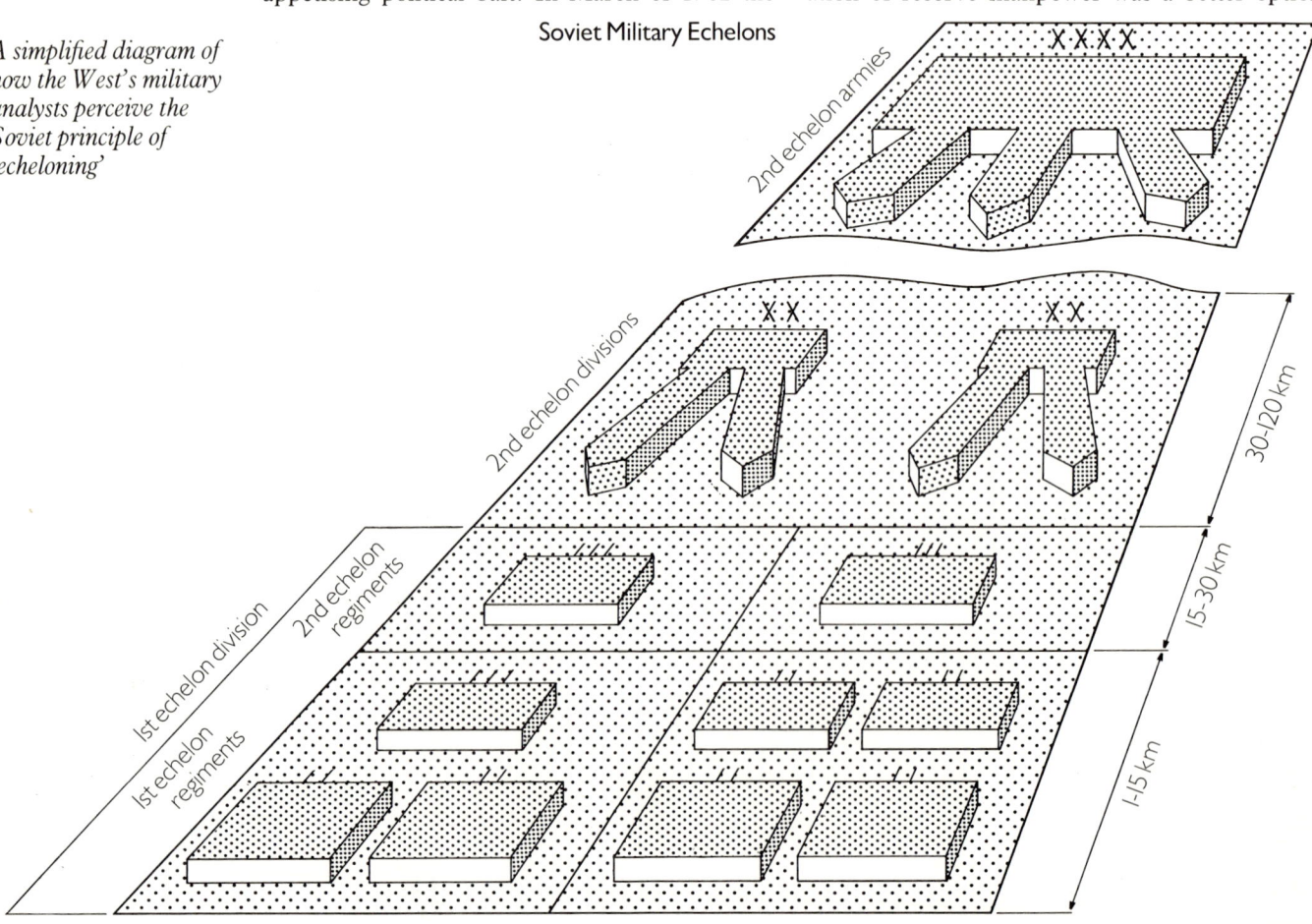

than high technology. Whether FOFA was based on a misreading of Soviet intentions in the first place. Whether FOFA did anything at all to raise the nuclear threshold. Whether the doctrine was overdependent on cripplingly expensive and untried technology. But the pot was stirred above all by the publication in 1982 of the US Army's new field manual FM 100-5 Operations, the US Army's 'capstone, how to fight manual' which made AirLand Battle the official warfighting doctrine of the US Army. At the same time the US Army Training and Doctrine Command, TRADOC, released AirLand Battle 2000, a futuristic study of the potential high technology battlefield of the years 1995–2015 which blended offensive manoeuvre and firepower in an even more lethally awe inspiring mix. The result was an immediate crossing of the confusion threshold with politicians and journalists struggling to disassemble one set of acronym-ridden proposals from another and official doctrine from concepts put up for discussion.

SACEUR himself tried to unscramble the mess. Writing in May 1983 he stated, 'The ACE concept for attacking Warsaw Pact follow on forces by conventional means should not be confused with the US Army's concepts of AirLand Battle and Airland Battle 2000. Airland battle is the official doctrine of the US Army set forth in the 1982 edition of FM 100-5 Operations. AirLand Battle 2000 has not yet been adopted as doctrine, but is an approved US Army concept that attempts to envisage how US forces might fight early in the 21st century. These useful US Army concepts were developed independently of ACE's initiatives or its concept of operations. The ACE concept is wholly an ACE, and hence a multinational product.' And General Rogers was later at pains to point out the vital differences in detail:

'We do not plan for the integrated use of conventional, nuclear and chemical weapons in ACE. We make a clear distinction between conventional and mass destruction weapons. Any use by the Alliance of either chemical or nuclear weapons would always be in accordance with release procedures approved by Alliance political authorities.

'We will not engage in pre-emptive strikes. NATO is a defensive Alliance and as such will never fire the first shot.

'Contrary to popular perception we will not attack across our borders with ground forces heading deep into the enemy's rear area. We will however use the counter-attack – the essence of a viable defence – to restore our borders.'

US National guardswomen train with an M60 machine gun

The concept of Follow on Forces Attack and that of AirLand Battle thus show major differences but, in spite of FM 100-5 being a manual with worldwide application, both are designed to provide the combat doctrine for war on a single set piece battlefield, central Europe, based on the developing threat and dispositions of a single enemy. How AirLand Battle and FOFA differ therefore is as important as their points of contact.

The US Army in Europe

Since the end of the Korean War, the disastrous distraction into Viet Nam notwithstanding, the attention of the armed forces of the United States has always been firmly fixed on Europe and on NATO's Central Sector in particular, the region where its forces physically confront the main body of its ideological enemy on the Inner German Border. The US Army may provide only a comparatively small proportion of NATO's ground forces in place but after full reinforcement the US finds 1·3 million out of a NATO total of 4·5 million, and of course when tactical nuclear weapons are included, the US Army and Air Force control the overwhelming proportion of its total firepower albeit under dual key control. Supreme Allied Commander Europe (SACEUR) is always an American soldier and the Commander in Chief of US Army Europe (USAREUR) is also the commander of NATO's Central Army Group (CENTAG). How NATO intends to conduct any war in Europe is thus of crucial concern to the United States and how America's armed forces plan to fight a war in Europe is of crucial concern to NATO's European nations.

AirLand Battle doctrine emphasises a return to the 'operational' level of war on the part of the defender, a level of warfare between tactics and strategy in which battles if not wars themselves are won. This is achieved by seizing the offensive initiative early and using ground manoeuvre forces and deep strike firepower to engage both the enemy forces already committed and the enemy's follow on forces not yet in contact. Throughout the AirLand battle doctrine the army corps commander is identified as the key rung of authority with an area of influence stretching 150 kilometres behind the front line. A deep battle in this area may be fought with manoeuvre forces, airmobile forces or firepower *including* nuclear firepower once release authority has been received. Airland Battle doctrine does not assume that nuclear release marks the end of coherent battlefield operations, in fact operations will continue on the integrated battlefield as long as necessary and must be planned for with nuclear fire support from the outset.

US Army M109 155mm self-propelled howitzer capable of throwing a nuclear or conventional shell up to 15 kilometres

The point must be made that understanding FM 100-5 and AirLand Battle as an American operations plan for war in Central Europe is not the whole story. AirLand Battle is a prescription for warfare up to the corps level of command. In the case of NATO these are subject to command at Army Group level (CENTAG and NORTHAG) of NATO Forces Central Europe (AFCENT) and ACE itself (Allied Command Europe) via which operational orders and any authorisation to use nuclear weapons by the national command authorities would flow. The 'victory' that AirLand Battle calls for, the destruction of the enemy's first operational echelon, is at the operational level of war, the art of winning battles as a part of winning wars, and thus a component of deterrent strategy which strives to make the political risks of attack unacceptable. The deep battle is again fought at the 'operational level' to a maximum depth of 150 kilometres behind the main battle area.

FOFA by contrast must be considered as a doctrine written around a particular set of circumstances, put simply, the basic way NATO plans to defend itself. It does not include deep attack by ground manoeuvre forces, nor deep strike with nuclear weapons outside the remit of flexible response. It does however envisage deep strike conventional firepower being used to engage hostile follow on forces across the whole depth of the enemy's array of forces as far as target acquisition and weapon system technology allows, reaching as far as garrison areas in the western military districts of the Soviet Union

Any army, whatever the level of its technology base and the subtlety of its doctrine makers, is made up of people – reflecting the strengths and weaknesses of the society it serves. The US Army has rebuilt its morale after the slough of Viet Nam but problems persist

itself, several hundred kilometres deep. At these kinds of ranges FOFA is much more clearly dependent on emerging technology to be able to look deep and strike deep with certainty than is AirLand Battle, which is really a new way of using assets already in place or shortly to be so.

FOFA as an accepted sub-concept of NATO operational doctrine and AirLand Battle as the official war fighting doctrine of the US Army, may sit uneasily within each other like crudely made Russian dolls but the important point is they are compatible within the minds of those who are tasked with carrying out the military defence of the West and within the minds of the politicians who must persuade their electorates to find the economic resources to pay for them. But the debate has not ended. The colossal research demands of military technology are as much about time as money – decisions taken today will show up as hardware decades hence and the development period will span the lifetimes of several governments. Like the Soviet Army, the arguments marshalled against FOFA and AirLand Battle are not going to go away.

EMERGING TECHNOLOGY:
A Revolution in War

'It was as natural as breathing for me to perceive that airpower would revolutionise war. It required no vision, no stretch of the imagination, but was merely a matter of seeing the obvious'

Basil Lidell Hart, *Memoirs, Volume 1*, 1965

In this century when weapon science has been pursued with an urgency and on a scale as great as any life enabling endeavour, the rate of change from one generation to another of weapon systems has been dramatic. The technology of modern weapon systems such as a combat aircraft, tank or guided missile can be traced back through recognisable generations to recognisable prototypes with an evolutionary pattern as the result - marked by peaks on the graph when the results of a breakthrough in pure science are engineered into what in effect must be a practical battlefield tool, advances such as lightweight alloys for aircraft in the 1920s, radar in the 1930s, jet engines in the 1940s, nuclear propulsion for warships in the 1950s and so on, and particularly when several of them are combined at once. The aspect of big science that is dominating the technology of weapons systems today, is like so much else, that of computer power and information technology – the marriage of machine intelligence with telecommunications. Weapon systems may not yet have artificial intelligence in the purest sense but they certainly might be said to have discriminatory intelligence, even to 'hold opinions', not whether this particular war may be worth fighting as soldiers are wont to consider but whether that source of heat emissions down there is the engine decking of a tank or a field kitchen.

The Americans, with a love of acronyms that sometimes confuses as much as clarifies, talk of 'VISTA' technologies – 'very intelligent surveillance and target acquisition', which is just that, through advanced sensor techniques and computer analysis of the results to impart to the weapon itself the ability to find and strike its target, rather than to its flesh and blood operator. VISTA is one of five technological thrusts being pursued by the US Army research and development effort. The remainder are: *distributed command, control and intelligence* (DC³I) to 'dramatically improve the distribution of battlefield intelligence among all levels of command', *self-contained munitions, soldier-machine interface* and *biotechnology*, to 'assist in the prevention and treatment of casualties through new classes of vaccines, antidotes and treatment compounds'.

Look Deep/Strike Deep

A weapon system equipped with an appropriate sensor and a certain amount of discriminatory intelligence can affect warfare in a fundamental way. It can be as effective hundreds of kilometres from its launch point as it could be if operated like a sniper's rifle in the front line. For a long time this has been true of missiles aimed against fixed targets where inertial guidance and simple ballistic calculations have been enough,

but VISTA technologies bring moving targets into the equation. In doing so they create a dilemma – should resources be allotted to sophisticated and therefore expensive weapons which can perform effectively deep behind the enemy's front line or to simpler yet equally 'smart' weapons which would have tremendous stopping power on the line of contact.

The military requirement to strike deep is as old as a slingshot, but always striving in fact to make the odds more favourable at the line of contact by wearing the enemy down before he got there. In the age when wars were decided by muscle power, the longbow presented an alternative to hacking away at each other with sword and axe. Bowmen could bring down armoured horsemen at seventy yards but the ones that got through would cut them to bits unless they were protected by pikemen. Gunpowder changed much but not everything. Frederick the Great's infantry opened fire with volleys of musketry at

100 paces from the enemy line before closing with the bayonet. Frederick's artillery gave direct fire support at 500 yards and 'howitzers' lobbed projectiles at high trajectories, striking at reserves hidden behind hills and trees, whose presence had been detected by cavalry scouts.

The nineteenth century technical revolution transformed firepower by introducing breech loading and automatic weapons to the battlefield with the added ingredient of telecommunications. The war of 1914–18 was fought with most of the new technology of battlefield mass destruction in place – but the western front co-agulated into trench warfare because the stopping power of machine guns was unbreakable by infantry assault and, which when implaced in defensive fortifications, were also largely immune to the deep strike systems of the day – massed siege artillery. Even the introduction of such radical technical innovations as poison gas and tanks brought their employers only localised advantages.

The First World War added the new dimension of air power to warfare. The primary role was reconnaissance, spotting targets for the long-range artillery – while fighters, bombers and ground attack aircraft evolved almost as a tactical afterthought. In terms of firepower, it was the co-operation of airman and artilleryman which mattered.

Above: This dramatic illustration shows the MW-1 weapon system of a West German Tornado at the moment of detonation, strewing sub-munitions over a wide area

Right: Another novel approach to the problem of deep attack is the expendable but 'smart' drone, programmed for example to attack air defence radars. This is the Boeing developed Robotic Airborne Vehicle

In the air/land battles of 1939–45 the tank reclaimed the primacy of the offensive with ground attack aircraft providing the fire support. Deeper ranging aircraft went for targets in the enemy rear, seeking to paralyse his command structure and his logistic ability to sustain the battle at the front line or bring up reserves. It was the ability of the aircraft to strike deep that let armoured formations dominate the battle-fields of the Blitzkrieg era.

Today's generation of combat aircraft has been developed around what are now the 'traditional' roles of tactical airpower. In broad terms these are counter-air warfare, intelligence gathering, close air support and interdiction.

Counter-air warfare embraces every aspect of the struggle for air superiority, that is winning control of airspace so that airpower can be brought to the aid of the land battlefield, either in attack or defence. Counter-air operations can be offensive or defensive, involving surface-to-air systems, air-to-air combat, suppression of electronic defences and most importantly, deep attacks on an enemy's support structure for waging war in the air – airfields, dispersed operating bases, air defence radars, airborne early warning aircraft and so on.

Close air support (CAS) is designed to apply precise and flexible firepower against enemy forces in direct contact or close to the front line of the battle.

Interdiction, like reconnaissance, requires the penetration of defended airspace to attack targets, the destruction of which will detract from the enemy's combat power at the front. Air interdiction is defined by the US Department of Defense as, 'air operations conducted to destroy, neutralize, or delay the enemy's military potential before it can be brought to bear effectively against friendly forces, at such distance from friendly forces that detailed integration of each air mission with the fire and movement of friendly forces is not required'.

The combat aircraft designed for interdiction and airfield attack is among the most expensive of individual weapon systems. It has to take its pilot to the target and therefore it has to be designed to penetrate hostile airspace bristling with surface-to-air missiles, radar nets and interceptor fighters, and come back. It has to fly low and fast so its airframe and avionics will be highly complex and expensive (like the RAF's Tornado GR 1 with variable-geometry wings and terrain-following radar). It will also have to

Above: The airfields of NATO and the Warsaw Pact would be critical targets in the opening moves of any war in Europe. USAF nuclear capable F-111s are based in Britain

Right: Like NATO, the fixed wing aircraft of the Warsaw Pact are tied to great rafts of concrete (the notable exception being the RAF and US Marine Corps Harriers). These are MiG-27 Floggers of Soviet Frontal Aviation

carry self protection devices such as anti-radar missiles and electronic jamming pods to increase its chances of survival while detracting from its own offensive weapons load.

The complexity and expense of the manned penetrating aircraft reflects a constant in the problems of striking deep, problems that are as old as warfare – the deeper the target the more complicated the system required to reach it and strike it with accuracy, the gathering of intelligence in hostile territory is always difficult and dangerous, fixed targets are easier to find and strike than moving ones and an efficient and vulnerable command, control and communications network is required to make it all work.

See Deep

To strike deep you have to see deep. The whole scope of the military intelligence gathering process is appropriate but this section concentrates upon the technology for battlefield surveillance by airborne radar. Suffice it to say that the ability to peer into an enemy's heartland, to read his dispositions and glean his intentions, has been transformed by the deployment of space-based reconnaissance satellites and the sophisticated techniques of electronic intelligence (Elint) gathering.

These techniques apply particularly to fixed targets such as bridges, river crossings, railway marshalling yards, road junctions, airfields and

Left: The British Army is developing a 'cut price' see deep system based on a purpose built drone called Phoenix and an airborne radar system dubbed Castor mounted in a twin turboprop light transport. Development is being conducted with a Britten-Norman Islander seen here in an airborne early warning configuration

Left: The Israeli Scout and Mastiff remotely-piloted vehicles showed their potential in the Lebanon fighting of 1982. Able to transmit reconnaissance TV pictures in real time the operational results were eagerly examined by US analysts

so on. To find and fix moving targets, however, a surveillance system that can locate and track them on the move, while transmitting the information in real time (that is as it happens) is needed. Here the problems begin to multiply. The surveillance system should be operable in all weathers and in the dark, it should be electronically subtle enough to peer through camouflage and weed out decoys and pick up moving target indications (MTI) from background radar clutter. Its data links should be invulnerable to electronic warfare and it should itself not have to venture into harm's way, leaving the penetration of hostile airspace to the weapon system for which it is finding targets.

The US Army began evaluating airborne battlefield surveillance radar in 1958 by converting eight Beech L-23E Seminole light transports into RL-23D radar reconnaissance aircraft, the first two with Motorola AN/APS 85 sideways-looking airborne radar (SLAR) and a further six with Texas Instruments UPD-1 AN/APQ-6 equipment in 1960. The UPD-1 installations pioneered the use of a real time data link to ground stations and a developed version, TI's UPD-2, was installed in the US Army's first operational electronic battlefield surveillance aircraft, the Grumman OV-1 Mohawk which was flown in prototype form in 1959.

The OV-1 has been developed through four models of which the OV-1D is the current, carrying as its primary sensor the APS-94 side-looking radar with a detection range of up to 100 kilometres or a down-looking infra-red mapper plus high resolution cameras, neither of which can transmit data while in flight.

Left: Grumman OV-10 Mohawk with sideways-looking battlefield surveillance radar

Ground surveillance radar in use by a US infantry unit

In the mid-1970s the US Army and Air Force began an effort to enhance their tactical reconnaissance capabilities from a largely clear weather force with an intelligence collection – processing – distribution cycle stretching into days, into an all-weather, automated, intelligence gathering system of great sophistication, peering deep into enemy territory and generating tactical information in near real time. Meanwhile the air force embarked upon the so-called Pave Strike programme to transform its capability to fly air-to-ground strike missions in all weathers and at night based on new technology first tested in Viet Nam (see later). Five of the eleven programmes under the Pave Strike umbrella were concerned with target detection and acquisition, including the Precision Location Strike System (PLSS) looked at in detail later.

The US Army meanwhile began development in the early 1970s of a system called SOTAS (Stand Off Target Acquisition System) which built on the battlefield surveillance technology used in the OV-1 but adding a moving target indicator and jam-proof, real time data links. SOTAS could have been mounted on piloted vehicles but was tested on helicopters, four UH-1 Hueys being converted in 1975 with a rotating plank antenna below the fuselage. The SOTAS helicopters were tested in Korea and West Germany where they were later permanently assigned while research and development continued at no small expense. The programme peaked in 1979 when the Army requested funds for sixty SOTAS-equipped UH-60 Blackhawk helicopters designated EH-60B. In fact only four were flown when continuing electronics problems slammed the independent Army programme to a halt and pushed the service into a shotgun marriage with the Air Force and its continuing deep surveillance programmes – thus was 'JSTARS', the Joint Surveillance and Target Attack Radar System born in 1982.

The USAF's development thrust for battlefield surveillance progressed through the 1970s on two distinct lines. During the Viet Nam War a programme designed to fix the positions of hostile missile-control radars had begun, codenamed Pave Onyx. This was developed into an Airborne Radar Location and Strike System (ALSS) which was tested in Europe in 1975 with the high-flying U-2C aircraft as the sensor platform. In 1977 Lockheed won the contract to develop an advanced version of the system called PLSS (Precision Location Strike System) able to pinpoint and determine the type of hostile 'emitters' deep within enemy territory (a figure of 322 kilometres has been quoted).

Originally, a high-altitude remotely-piloted vehicle was considered as a platform for PLSS but when the ambitious USAF Compass Cope RPV

programme was cancelled, the unique qualities of the original U-2 spyplane, with its ability to operate at very high altitude for long loiter times, were once again called upon. Lockheed re-engineered the design and re-opened production lines to produce the TR-1. This was characterised by two large wing pods housing the electronic equipment and had an operational ceiling of 90 000 feet or over 27 kilometres, and a mission endurance of 12 hours. As currently invisaged PLSS would be used operationally by groups of three TR-1s, each flying race track patterns at high altitude within friendly air space. The crucial data on hostile emitters is transmitted via jam-proof downlinks to ground control stations.

PLSS can count as an electronic warfare programme, the source of its target information being the emissions of hostile transmitters, and thus can equate with a 'traditional' air force air defence suppression role. The US Air Force was also anxious to get into the moving target acquisition and strike business and was developing in parallel a programme called WAAM (Wide Area Anti-armour Munitions). This began in 1975 with an advanced target acquisition element codenamed Pave Mover, capable of distinguishing moving targets against background clutter and designating for robotic weapon systems to home in on at ranges well beyond the forward edge of the battle area.

In 1978 the Army and Air Force programmes were shunted together under the auspices of the Defense Advanced Research Projects Agency under an umbrella technology proving programme called Assault Breaker. A joint executive committee with representatives from the Department of Defense and the two services was set up to look at the broad policy issues while a joint steering committee was to supervise the transition from technology demonstration to the development of prototype hardware. From the beginning the progress of Assault Breaker was going to be difficult, technical considerations

US Army technician tends the electronics of an OV-1 Mohawk battlefield surveillance aircraft. The Motorola APS-94D radar with two sideways-looking antennae can map an area up to 100 km either side of the aircraft with a range control selecting 25, 50 or 100 km wide scans by each antenna

Assault Breaker

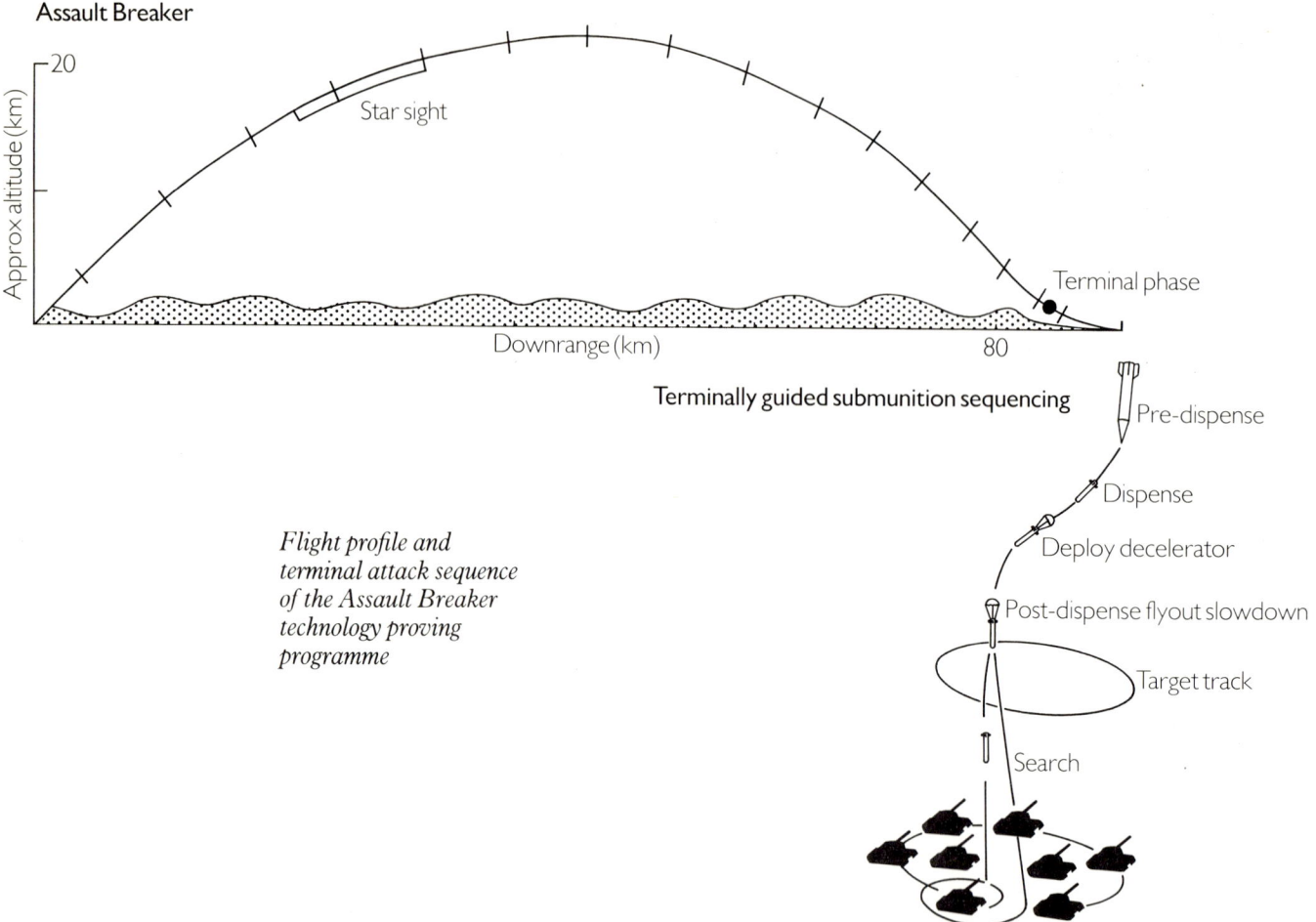

*Flight profile and
terminal attack sequence
of the Assault Breaker
technology proving
programme*

aside, with the Air Force responsible for the target acquisition component and the Army initially responsible for the main strike component in the shape of the Corps Support Weapon System (CSWS) looked at in detail later. It was also recognised that the radar component, the key to the whole concept, was going to be the most difficult to engineer. It would have to identify worthwhile targets, track them on the move, provide continuous guidance to a number of missiles simultaneously, steering them towards the target arrays it had identified and itself avoiding detection and jamming. In February 1981 the US General Accounting Office estimated Assault Breaker's cost at $5300 million for a programme designed to equip two US Corps in USAREUR – broken down as $130 million for technology demonstration, $510 million for development and production of five Pave Mover units, $4·225 million for the Corps Support Weapon System and $390 million for equivalent air-launched, stand-off anti-armour missiles.

Development contracts for the Pave Mover TAWDS (Target Acquisition Weapon Delivery System) were issued in 1979, Hughes and Grumman/Norden producing prototypes in 1981. Both were sideways-looking radars installed in an F-111A airframe with antennas approximately 3·5 metres long feeding information into a powerful onboard computer. Both types proved capable of tracking up to six target arrays simultaneously, each typically a formation of up to 12 tanks, and able to transmit guidance updates to two missiles in flight. However, the ability to distinguish between high value main battle tanks and soft skin vehicles was not engineered into the system in an effort to compress development time, while the test conditions during initial experiments at White Sands proving range were not conducted in simulated electronic warfare conditions but in an environment officially described by the US Army as 'benign'.

Once again the Air Force and Army programmes were pushed together when in May 1982 the Assault Breaker technology proving programme became Joint Stars with the Air Force as lead service for the 'see deep' surveillance requirement, the Army retaining the missile now named the Joint Tactical Missile System or JTACMS. It was originally intended that the Joint Stars radar should go aloft in Army OV-1 Mohawks reporting to Corps HQ and Air Force TR-1s or C-18s, however in May 1984 the programme was reconfigured yet again with the Air Force becoming the sole operator with the system projected for installation in 15 C-18s, airframes reworked from former Boeing 707-323 civil transports.

Strike Deep

The second component of the Assault Breaker technology proving programme was the weapon system itself, designed to attack mobile targets deep behind the front line, typically second echelon armour. The US Air Force in 1975 had begun the Wide Area Anti-armour Munitions (WAAM) programme to improve the prospects for air attack against armour (by a factor of eight in a single pass). It also had a programme for an air-launched missile which could be launched at long range against deep targets without the carrier aircraft having to penetrate hostile airspace (the Conventional Stand-off Weapon or CSW). The Army meanwhile had the Corps Support Weapon System, a surface-to-surface missile capable of delivering nuclear, anti-personnel, anti-armour, chemical and terminally-guided payloads at greater ranges and with greater accuracy than the existing Lance missile. For Assault Breaker two competing missiles were developed, Martin Marietta's T-16 based on the Patriot SAM and Vought's T-22 based on the Lance but incorporating major improvements including a solid-fuel motor and navigation via ring-laser gyros which conferred a sixfold increase in accuracy. This was demonstrated on the T-22's first flight when it impacted within 25 metres of the aiming point after a flight of 64 kilometres. The T-16's guidance system is no less sophisticated, using stellar inertial navigation which takes a star shot in mid-course to update its computerised guidance.

But these were just the delivery systems – it was what they were carrying which made the Assault Breaker programme potentially so important – terminally-guided submunitions.

Left: Extended range Anti-armour Munition (ERAM), a 'smart' mine which can be air delivered along an enemy avenue of approach for example. On activation the ERAM dispenses two Skeet warheads

Above: 'Top attack' in action. The armour protection of a tank is thinnest on top and this is why smart submunitions such as Skeet are configured to attack from above

Terminal guidance is the system which steers a missile to its target in the last stages of its flight. In an anti-ship or long-range air-to-air missile for example, the mid-course stage is directed by inertial guidance, a system of gyroscopes and accelerometers which keeps the missile on a pre-programmed heading. In the closing stages, its own onboard system cuts in, typically a short-range radar which picks up the echo of its own emissions from the target aircraft or ship and homes in on them. The simplest form of terminal guidance relies on the target's own emissions in the form of heat and for many years infra-red seekers have been used in short-range surface-to-air or air-to-air missiles. Tanks on the move equally are emitters of heat, especially from the engine decking which in traditional tank design has been the least protected

Above: Skeet 'smart' warhead. It has an infra-red sensor which detects heat sources below it and a self forging fragment which propels a slug of very dense material moving at very high velocity at an armoured target from above

Left: Skeets can be packaged into all sorts of delivery systems including Avco's Sensor Fuzed Weapon submunition configured for delivery from strike aircraft flying fast and low

Far left: Test launch of the Martin Marietta T-16, an original candidate for the Corps Support Weapon System submunition-carrying deep strike system

part of the tank's armoured carapace, the heavy armour being reserved for the frontal area to face other tanks and infantry weapons.

Two types of terminally-guided submunitions were tested – the General Dynamics developed TGSM and the Avco Skeet. The General Dynamics system used a two-colour infra-red seeker with special filters to screen out decoys. It is designed to be dispensed in any one of four patterns, two of which are circles of 250 or 350 metres or ellipses 400 or 800 metres long to attack armour in line of march. The right pattern would be determined by the analysis of the target determined by the Pave Mover radar. As it approaches the target at a height of approximately 2000 metres, the carrier rocket performs a 'dispense manoeuvre', the outer skin panels are blasted free and the TGSMs are ejected by hydraulic plungers. Four seconds after release, the TGSM deploys its own parachute and folding wings spring out to give it lift for manoeuvring. Six seconds later the seeker activates, beginning its search for hot targets below.

The Skeet system uses a sub-submunition technique. Each 'Skeet Delivery Vehicle' fits into the same space as the TGSM but itself contains four 'Skeets' each weighing 2·7 kg. The SDVs are dispensed at a height of 3000 metres and deploy tail fins for stability as they descend. A parachute now deploys at 200 metres, power is supplied to the individual Skeets and their infra-red seekers are cooled. At 30 metres the parachute is released and a peripheral rocket motor spins the SDV anti-clockwise at 3000 rpm, forcing the tail fins to close up again and shooting out pairs of spinning Skeets. As they are ejected a spring-loaded arm pops up causing the Skeet to wobble, enlarging its search pattern. When a target has been detected the Skeet's 6·5 kg warhead detonates to produce a 'self forging' fragment turning a chunk of heavy metal such as depleted uranium into a streamlined projectile travelling at very high speed penetrating armour by kinetic energy with deadly effect.

Weapons Against Fixed Targets

As it stands today, only manned aircraft are capable of carrying out NATO's interdiction mission by conventional means. The dual-capable Lance missile is only accurate to within 375 metres at its maximum range of 125 kilometres. The Pershing Ia and Pershing II ballistic missiles are nuclear-capable systems only. Fixing interdiction choke points such as river crossings is relatively straightforward but penetrating through SAM-belts and defended airspace is not. The USAF plans to fly 'composite' missions through defended airspace with strike aircraft accompanied by specialised electronic warfare aircraft such as F-4G Wild Weasel and EF-111A Raven to directly attack and degrade the enemy defences, plus escorting air superiority fighters.

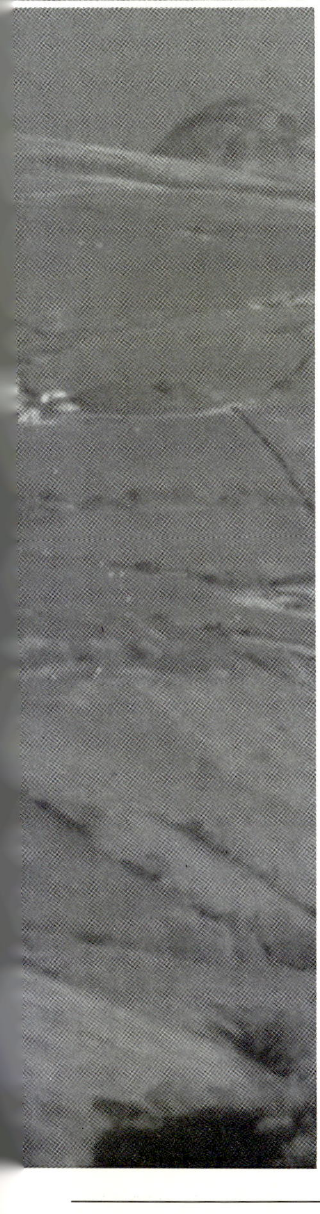

Manned penetrating aircraft remain the most effective means to bring deep mobile targets under threat but ever more sophisticated air defences makes them increasingly vulnerable. USAFE has deployed the EF-111A electronic warfare aircraft (above) as an escort for deep strike aircraft

Left: F-111 variable geometry deep interdictor aircraft designed to fly fast and low evading hostile air defence radars. Below: General Dynamics F-16, designed as an air combat fighter but capable of lifting a formidable load of strike weapons including free fall nuclear bombs

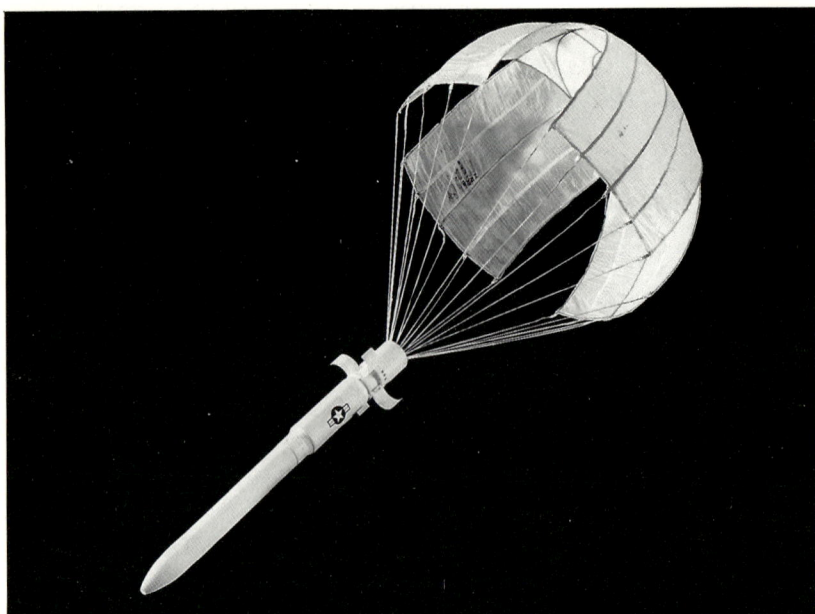

Concrete runways may be sprawlingly vulnerable but they are in fact quite hard to knock out by conventional bombing. Avco's prototype Direct Airfield Attack Combined Munitions packages eight runway cratering munitions (seen left with parachute deployed) inside a standard USAF tactical munitions dispenser. There are also twenty-four area denial mines designed to hinder attempts at repair

European NATO air forces put more faith in two-ship, below the radar operations made by high performance aircraft such as the RAF's Tornado GR 1 but these must be engineered for independent operations in all weathers and at night and for target acquisition and weapon delivery at high speed and at low level where line of sight, precision guidance techniques such as laser designation become inoperable. At present free-fall area munitions such as cluster bombs are the most effective option but they still require overflying the target. It is not surprising therefore that all the relevant NATO air forces are increasingly looking to stand-off missile systems, again with some form of autonomous terminal guidance, to avoid having to overfly heavily defended target areas. It is a short step from an air-launched stand-off missile to a system which dispenses with the hugely expensive 'platform' represented by the aircraft and its pilot altogether, moving towards more cost efficient ground-launched missile systems which could perform the time critical interdiction mission against fixed targets. Here, however, NATO's nuclear conundrum once again raises its head. A ballistic missile used over intermediate range has a flight time of minutes. Once launched it is not recallable. Basing a deterrent posture on something indistinguishable from a nuclear delivery system is attended by grave problems.

Airfield attack presents a similar set of problems. The battle for air superiority is crucial to the outcome of the land battle for without it, Soviet Frontal Aviation can not only protect its own deep assets but also strike deep into NATO's rear, destroying its ability to reinforce and, crucially, destroying nuclear storage sites

and delivery systems by conventional means. NATO could rapidly exhaust its stock of surface-to-air missiles and see its interceptor force worn away by simple attrition by a numerically far stronger opponent. The classic formula for winning air superiority is not to battle it out in gallant dog fights but to get in first and catch the enemy on the ground.

Again the nuclear dilemma which attends the time critical, interdiction mission rears its ugly head, but more so. As it stands, the primary conventional means of attacking the Warsaw Pact's 35 to 40 main operating bases (MOBs) is once again the manned penetrating aircraft and even though equipped with a variety of specialised airfield attack munitions, the predictability of getting through to the target becomes more and more problematic. Hence there have been numerous proposals for turning the main operating base airfield attack mission over to guided missiles, thus freeing manned aircraft to go for the dispersed secondary operating bases choked with aircraft returning from the first wave. In the same way aircraft freed by missile attack from the interdiction mission could go for the mobile forces building up along wrecked communications and behind blocked choke points.

USAF Europe airfields would be among the very first targets should the use of chemical or nuclear weapons be sanctioned. This airman is wearing a full NBC suit on a peacetime exercise at a US airbase in Europe

The candidate systems proposed have been adaptations of both cruise and ballistic missile programmes. The USAF had a programme called MRASM (Medium-Range Air-to-Surface Missiles) based on the technology of the Tomahawk cruise missile but adapted for air launch and configured to fly along runways dispensing cratering submunitions. MRASM was cancelled in 1983 due to cost and inter-service incompatability. The ballistic missiles proposed are no less fearsome. CAM-40 is a proposed single-stage adaptation of the US Army's Pershing II, retaining the nuclear missile's radar area correlation guidance system and thus high accuracy. From bases in West Germany the missile could cover the majority of the Warsaw Pact's main and dispersed operating bases. The system would re-enter at twelve times the speed of sound and deliver a cluster of 24 kinetic energy penetrators fused to explode beneath the runway. Three CAM-40s would be required to scrub out a runway totally. The Lockheed project Axe used a Trident booster capable of long-range attack as an airfield smasher. The Trident has also been proposed for a system called Boss (Ballistic Offensive Suppression System) which envisages large delta-wing gliders swooping vengefully on the target airfield with eight clusters of concrete-chewing submunitions. At the very top of the fantasy curve is a system dubbed TABAS or Total Airbase Attack System with no less than a Saturn rocket as its booster, earning it the Army nickname 'Incredible Hulk'. The 25-tonne kinetic energy penetrator payload would be able to take out an entire airbase in one cataclysmic (but non-nuclear) attack.

The problem is therefore that to have a chance of winning the conventional battle on the ground, NATO needs to win air superiority. That in turn requires offensive counter-air strikes against airfields deep in Warsaw Pact territory, a mission currently slated for manned penetrating aircraft. Even as it stands these are dual-capable, able to deliver conventional or nuclear weapons, but turning over the mission to ballistic missiles with their critically short flight times, or indeed to slower moving cruise missiles which on a radar screen might look just the same as nuclear-armed versions, might do very little to enhance the Alliance's deterrent posture and even less to the prospects of raising the nuclear threshold.

Right: The HB 786 area denial munition is part of the British developed JP 233 airfield attack system designed to hold up repairs once runway cratering submunitions have done their work

Below: The French Durandal airfield attack weapon under test on a USAF Phantom. Like JP 233, such direct attack weapons require the strike aircraft to overfly heavily defended targets

High Technology and the Direct Battle

The technology that makes it possible to fight a deep battle with robotic weapons is also set to transform that fought in the zone of contact – indeed there are many analysts of NATO's defence posture who argue that this is where the technological and spending effort should go. If it means producing less flamboyantly dramatic weapons then so be it – what are needed are the resources to stop the massive armoured machine in its tracks where it matters – at the point of breakthrough, while computer simulated studies of Warsaw Pact forces' rear area activities point to the conclusion that daylight target opportunities in the first 30 kilometres behind the front line could outnumber all those, day or night, at greater depth. Resources, so it is argued, should be applied to short-range tactical systems, concentrating on increasing their rates of fire and ability to bring down destructive force with lethal accuracy while designing them to function

round the clock at night or in bad weather.

The problem of sheer numbers is daunting. On any one breakthrough front the Soviet Army could be expected to mass over 500 main battle tanks and as many infantry fighting vehicles with self-propelled artillery and self-mobile SAMs and anti-aircraft artillery in support – the sort of figures which make the prospect of abandoning tactical nuclear weapons so hard for NATO to embrace.

Meanwhile Soviet doctrine has not stood still. The lessons of the 1973 war when wire-guided anti-tank missiles in the hands of Egyptian infantry roughly handled Israeli tanks were keenly analysed within the Soviet Army. Massing more tanks was not the answer, on a breakthrough front they would just present a better target for area weapons (including nuclear weapons). Developing doctrine therefore further emphasised the bypassing of defences (rather than frontal assault), plus speed and surprise –

TOW launcher. Development of the US Army's standard heavy anti-tank missile began in 1965 and initial operational capability was reached in 1970. It was used in Viet Nam and the 1973 Middle East war and over a quarter of a million rounds have been manufactured

while technical innovations such as compound armour provided a short-term answer to the threat of current generation frontal attack weapons. Artillery and anti-aircraft support were beefed up while motor rifle battalions have been integrated into tank regiments to give infantry support. Thus the tank remains at the heart of the Soviet Army's combat power and NATO's primary front line target. The burden of the technological thrust is how to defeat it.

As far as NATO is concerned the answer lies in precision guidance – applying the smart solution to traditional and not so traditional weapon systems to increase dramatically their chances of actually striking and destroying their targets. As the technology proving programmes stand today, smartness is being engineered into just about everything from 20 mm cannon shells that can manoeuvre in flight, via mortars, infantry-portable anti-tank missiles, tube artillery, multiple rocket launchers, mines, and air-to-surface weapons launched by fixed-wing aircraft and helicopters. Main battle tanks are being put into the front line with fire-control equipment that would shame a battleship while anti-tank helicopters have become one of the most complex and expensive of individual weapon systems, dripping with target acquisition and designation equipment. Once again, as with the deep strike systems, the United States has overwhelming dominance in the technology and the actual production programmes.

Precision Guidance for Infantry Weapons

Infantry-operated anti-tank guided weapons (ATGWs) have come a long way since the first relatively crude generation of the mid-1950s which required outstanding soldierly skills to be effective. The developmental thrust is towards true 'fire-and-forget' weapons by employing the same millimetre wave and imaging infra-red seeker head technology base as the terminally-guided submunitions configured for deep strike weapons and, designing them with the ability to make so-called 'top attacks' on enemy armoured fighting vehicles where the armour is thinnest. Both the TOW and Dragon missiles which represent the US Army's standard current and medium-range anti-tank missiles employ semi-automatic to line-of-sight guidance in which the operator has to keep the cross hairs of his sight centred on the target, guidance controls being automatically generated and transmitted to the missile in flight via trailing wires to bring it into the operator's line of sight.

Dragon in particular has not been an unqualified success in service. Training devices have not been able to convey the sense of actually firing the missile which has been described as a 'bruising experience'. The operator is instructed to hold his breath during the missile's 12-second flight time and not to blink when the motor fires. The launcher must also be held down tightly on the shoulder lest the instinct to raise the shoulder on launch should send the missile into the ground.

The original Dragon replacement programme called for fire-and-forget capability from the beginning. Several development contracts were issued in 1980 around a 'mission element needs statement' for a shoulder-fired weapon weighing under 25 kg, operable day and night, with a 2000-metre range and a warhead capable of defeating new-generation Soviet tanks with compound armour. Meanwhile a separate technology demonstration programme was launched under DARPA auspices to prove technology much further down the risk curve. While the US Army very soon cancelled the original Dragon replacement programmes because of the bulk and weight of the weapons proposed, the DARPA programme, called Tank Breaker, offered the prospect of putting a lightweight and highly effective weapon in the hands of infantry platoons by incorporating a quantum jump in technology.

The key to Tank Breaker is the seeker head which uses a 'staring' focal plane array to detect and track hot targets, rather than a mechanically-scanning infra-red seeker. It is thus much lighter and less unwieldly than the generation of ATGWs it might replace. The focal plan seeker allows the operator to acquire and lock onto a target in daylight, darkness or the fog of battle. Once sighted and fired, the missile's own onboard computer steers it towards the target and the operator can himself disengage immediately. Following launch for a long-range mission the missile's autopilot steers it up to a cruise height of 150 metres. When the change in line of sight to the target as viewed by the seeker becomes ever more rapid, indicating that it is getting closer and closer, the missile will dive onto the upper surface of the target.

One of the candidate systems for the original Dragon replacement was to be a laser beam rider. Laser designation is now a mature technology based on original operational experience that came out of the air war over Viet Nam. Laser-guided bombs (LGBs) had their first successful trials at the USAF Armament Development and Test Center at Eglin AFB in 1966 – thus began the Paveway project with Texas Instruments as prime contractor developing add-on guidance kits for the USAF's standard free-fall bombs. Laser designation works by directing a pencil-thin beam of laser energy from a designator which may be installed in an aircraft, a remotely-piloted vehicle, a ground vehicle or in

Laser designators give the infantryman in the front line the ability to carry an artillery barrage if not quite in his pocket, then on his back. Using the Hughes Ground / Vehicular Laser Locator designator shown here, the operator uses the telescopic sight to scan for 'hard' targets such as tanks or bunkers. The laser not only provides range and bearing data but can 'sparkle' the target with coded pulses of energy on which laser homing weapons such as Copperhead shells or Paveway bombs can home

New generation air defence equipment for the US Army has been under development since the mid 1970s. The Patriot surface-to-air missile (below) entered limited production in 1980, warhead can be conventional or nuclear. The 'Sergeant York' *tracked divisional air defence gun was intended to give anti-aircraft protection to mobile US Army units. Because of cost overruns and technical shortcomings the programme collapsed in 1985 amid much controversy*

the hands of infantry. A target thus 'sparkled' will reflect laser energy on a pulsed and coded frequency, radiating like a beacon for any weapon system which has a laser seeker in its nose. In the beginning that meant free-fall bombs of the Paveway variety allowing infantry in close contact with the enemy to call up close air support which could be delivered with precision accuracy. Today, however, the number of laser-guided weapons has grown to include powered air-to-ground munitions, helicopter anti-tank missiles and artillery shells while the important laser designators are in the hands of infantry, in helicopters, on fixed-wing aircraft and, experimentally at least, on remotely-piloted vehicles such as the Lockheed Aquila.

Above: Wind tunnel model of the Tank Breaker missile developed by Hughes Aircraft for the US Army with a focal-plane array imaging infra-red seeker affording it a 'fire-and-forget' capability

Left: Hughes Modular Universal Laser Equipment (known as MULE), laser designator and rangefinder

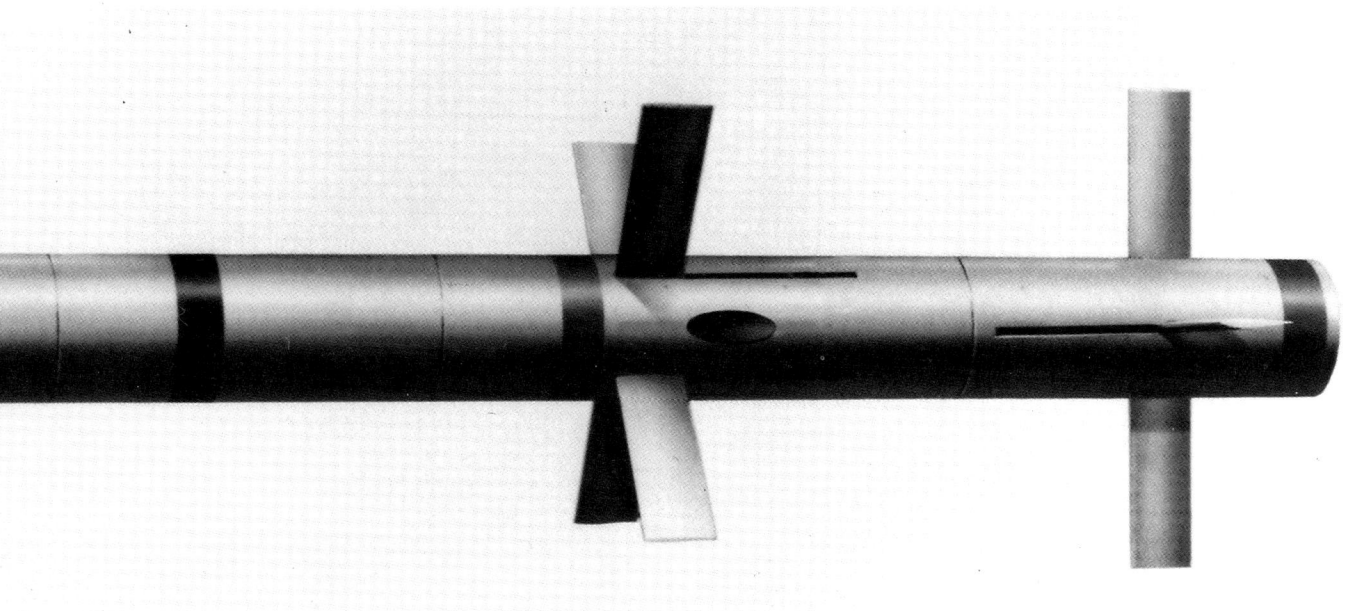

Smart artillery

Artillery has always meant warfare by numbers and computers have transformed the speed and accuracy of ballistic computation. Parallel advances in target acquisition and ammunition have made tube artillery a contender in the precision deep strike game – out to ranges of 30 kilometres at least, as well as giving direct fire support at the front line. Soviet towed artillery was being credited with ranges beyond 30 kilometres by the early 1970s, effectively outranging NATO's nuclear artillery with a conventional counterpart.

The technology of tube artillery has developed along four lines – increasing the range by advances in ordnance and ammunition, increases in lethality by applying precision terminal guidance to artillery shells which may incorporate submunitions, increasing co-ordinated firepower by computerised fire-control and communications and increasing tactical flexibility by emphasising self-propelled mountings.

The US Army has made strenuous efforts in pursuit of ever greater range for its tube artillery characterised by the provision of longer barrels for 155 mm and 8-inch guns, new high energy propellants, rocket-assisted projectiles and ballistically exotic ammunition while a programme called AFIS (Advanced Indirect Fire System) undertaken in the late 1970s foresaw ramjet-assisted projectiles with ranges of 70 kilometres and more equipped with 'fire-and-forget' terminal guidance. The M549 155 mm high explosive rocket-assisted projectile (RAP) round is less ambitious with a range of 30 kilometres while the M650 8-inch round has a solid propellant rocket

motor which burns for four seconds, igniting seven seconds after firing, also with a range of 30 kilometres (extreme range with unassisted projectiles is 24·3 kilometres). There are penalties in the quest for extreme range such as the effects of hot burning, high pressure charges on barrel life and the blast overpressure effects on the crew, and as ranges increase accuracy falls away and absolute dispersion increases. Precision guidance therefore, for example by laser designation, becomes attractive – but how to effect this 30 kilometres from the front line?

The second technological thrust therefore has been towards 'Improved Conventional Munitions' (ICM) a long-term high priority US Army programme to develop terminally-guided and cargo-carrying projectiles and thus increase lethality either by being certain of striking the target or spreading destructive effects over a wide area. Copperhead is one result, a 'cannon-launched guided projectile' or CLGP, destined, after a few bumpy years of mixed results in field trials and resulting political suspicion, to be procured in large numbers for the US and some NATO armies. As originally conceived the M712 Copperhead is an anti-armour weapon for fighting the direct battle at ranges between three and 16 kilometres. While conventional artillery in past wars has accounted for two-thirds of battlefield personnel casualties but only one per cent of tank kills, the M712 is designed to engage distant armoured targets by indirect fire with a high kill probability, just one or two rounds doing the job of 250 non-guided rounds. Laser guidance is the key, the M712 incorporating a laser seeker in the nose designed to acquire the

LHX: *Battlefield rotary wing fighters*

The armed helicopter has come a long way from the first lash ups used in counter insurgency war in the 'fifties and 'sixties. The US Army pioneered the development of tank killing machines designed to fly and fight at the heart of a high intensity battlefield like the AH-1 Huey Cobra and the Soviets responded with such formidable machines as the Mi-24 Hind, described as a 'low speed, rotary wing ground attack aircraft' rather than just another helicopter. The US Army also pioneered in Viet Nam the use of airmobile units, manpower and weapons flown into and out of the combat zone by helicopter there to fight dismounted and FM 100-5 prescribes doctrine for the use of 'air cavalry' in all kinds of tactical situations, in covering forces for example in the defence, in seizing defiles and crossing obstacles in exploiting the attack 'capitalising on their mobility to attack and cut off disorganized enemy units'.

An airborne armour-killing force which will not work in the dark or the rain is pretty useless and this is why the US Army has invested so much in the Hughes (now McDonnell Douglas Helicopters from mid 1985) AH-64A Apache, a supersophisticated attack helicopter with advanced all-weather sensors and night vision devices, armed with laser-guided missiles. Paralleling Apache deployment, the Army is acquiring large numbers of Sikorsky UH-60A Black Hawk helicopters for its airmobile units and both types will remain in service well into the next century.

Beyond the Apache and Black Hawk programmes lies an enormous procurement programme called LHX (Light Helicopter Experimental) designed to provide the US Army with up to 5000 combat machines for the opening decades of the next century. LHX on present plans would come in two basic configurations, a light utility version designated LHX-U and light scout attack designated LHX-SCAT. Beyond that LHX might not be a conventional helicopter at all with tailless, compound, tilt wing and advancing blade configurations being proposed. The missions which LHX might be called on to undertake include transport of up to eight troops, scout, ground attack and anti-tank, air defence suppression, engineer support, artillery observation, electronic warfare and rear area operations.

It is proposed that LHX should be single pilot operated with advanced electronics easing the considerable problems of flying terrain – following 'nap of the earth' missions in the dark while engaging multiple ground targets. The technology proving programme has already begun and is called ARTI (advanced rotorcraft technology integration), the purpose of which is to explore technologies which will make single pilot operation possible. In addition advanced powerplant and composite material technology is being explored in parallel programmes. LHX is also likely to carry self protective armament against hostile air threats, possibly in the shape of Stinger heat-seeking missiles adapted for air-to-air anti-helicopter operations.

*Bell Helicopters concept
for a single seat, tank
killing LHX*

Left: Copperhead launch from M198 155mm howitzer. Maximum range is up to 16 kilometres

Below: Copperhead cutaway. Behind the laser seeking head is a shaped charge warhead. The rear portion is the control section while wings and fins flip out after launch

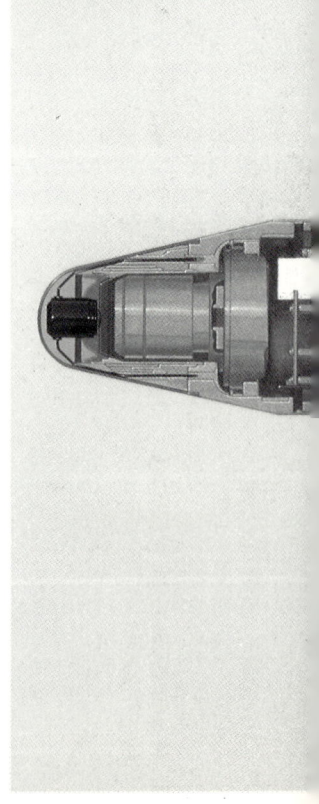

pulse-coded signature of a target 'painted' by a ground or airborne observer in the manner of a laser-guided bomb. The observer must have a clear line of sight to the target and calls for the firing of a Copperhead. The round is launched in an inert state. The acceleration then activates the battery which in turn powers up the onboard computer and autopilot while the aerodynamic control surfaces flip out. The observer illuminates the target for the last ten seconds of the Copperhead's flight while the seeker nose picks up the laser pulses and generates instructions for the control surfaces to steer the round unerringly onto the target. One of the Copperhead's shortcomings in early tests was the laser seeker's inability to operate below the kind of cloud base levels obtaining for much of the time in northern Europe. However a technique known as trajectory shaping allows the round to fly a semi-ballistic flight path under the specified 3000 feet (914 metres). A 'fly under, fly out' trajectory controlled by the projectile's own onboard computer allows for the engagement of targets beyond eight kilometres in bad weather where the Copperhead travels at lower altitude to provide a longer time beneath cloud ceilings.

Cargo-carrying artillery shells have been developed in tandem, able to engage enemy forces directly by dispensing smart submunitions or by creating mine or area denial barriers. Thirdly they can be used to disperse autonomous reconnaissance sensors. The basic carrier shell of the US Army, ballistically compatible with other 155 mm improved conventional munitions, is the M483A1 which contains 88 miniaturised dual-purpose submunitions for anti-armour or anti-personnel wide area attack. A significant development of the technique is called SADARM (Sense and Destroy Armour) which allies the cargo-carrying shell concept to terminally-guided submunitions. In the initial concept for SADARM using an 8-inch M509 as the carrier, submunitions are dispensed over the target area by time fuze, descending by parachute with a millimetric wave sensor scanning a 75-metre radius cone beneath them. If a target is located a warhead of the self-forging fragment (SFF) type is detonated attacking the thinner top armour. SFFs are a combination of the kinetic energy and high explosive anti-tank (HEAT) warheads used in conventional anti-tank munitions. A shaped hollow charge of high explosive is used, faced by a plate of a very dense material such as depleted uranium. On detonation the

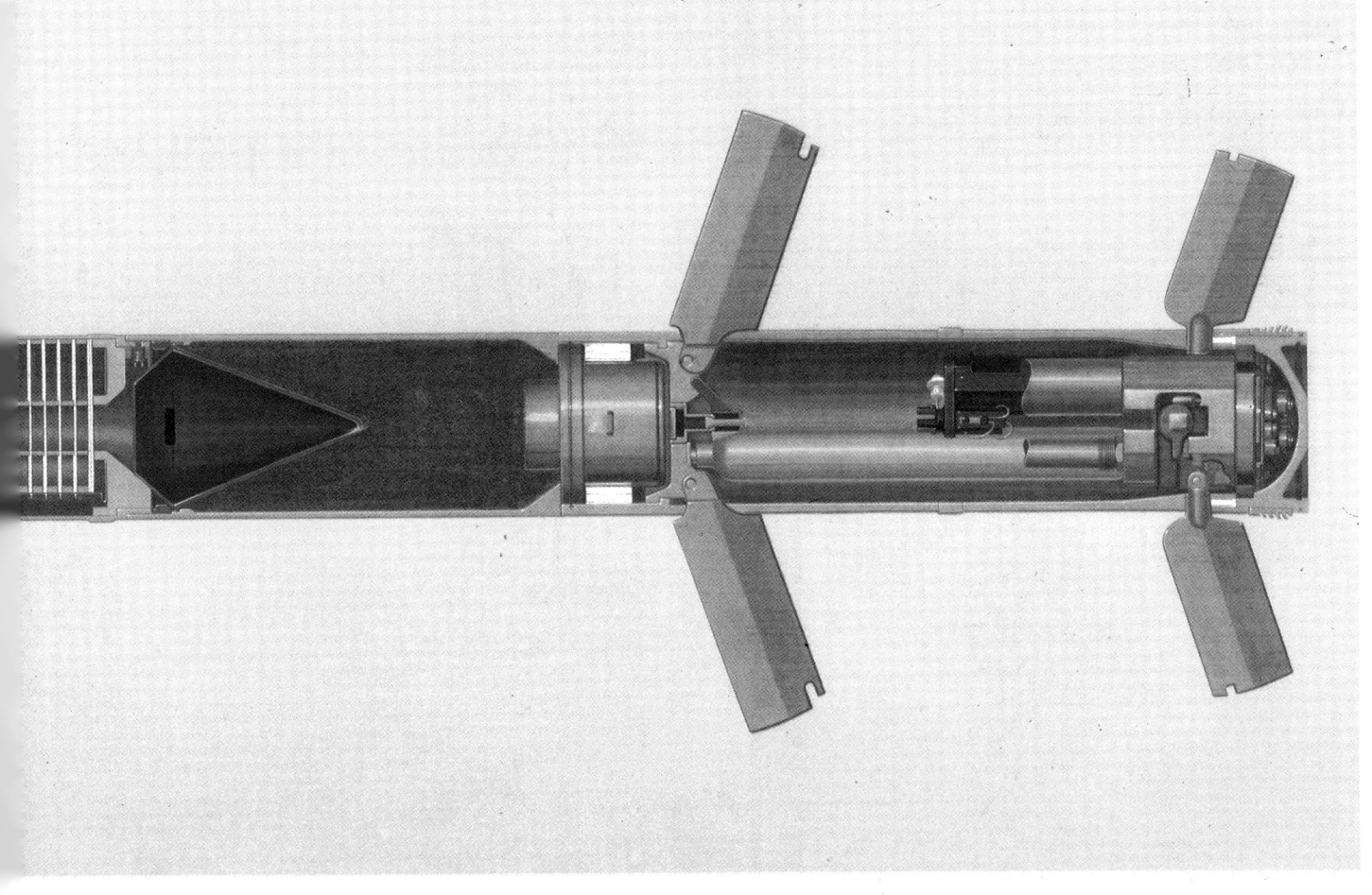

metal forms a ballistically-shaped slug moving at very high velocity, enough to crack open a tank's turret or engine decking from above. The technique is also used in the so-called Enhanced Sensing Munition, or ESM, also derived from the ubiquitous Avco Skeet, employed in a system called Improved Remote Area Anti-Armor Mine or IRAAM which has opened up the usefulness of tube artillery in being able to lay anti-armour or anti-personnel mine barriers rapidly. By packaging six IRAAMs in an M438A1 carrier shell, a 155 mm SADARM round is the result, designated XM898. In this role the Skeet can either attack from above or fall to the ground where it waits as a mine with sensors activated for the target to come to it.

Tube artillery launched mines came under another umbrella programme called FASCAM (Family of Scatterable Mines) which also embraces helicopter and fixed-wing aircraft sowed systems and a ground-based system called GEMSS which sows mines from a trailer towed behind wheeled or tracked vehicles, punching them out at preset 30-metre intervals. The ability to lay down mine barriers quickly and at stand-off range if necessary, is regarded as being of great tactical significance for bringing new pace to the battlefield both in attack and defence.

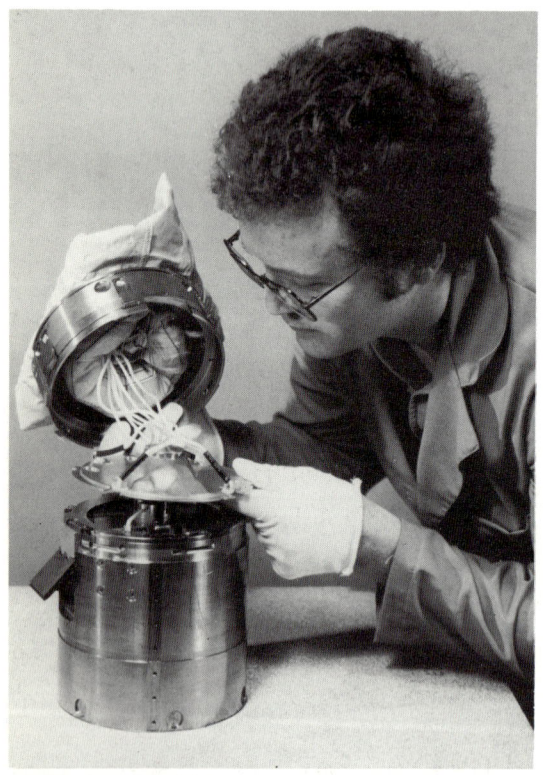

Above: The SADARM submunition ('sense and destroy armour') with its pre-packed parachute

Right: US M110A2 203mm self-propelled howitzer can fire submunition rounds

Multiple Rocket Launchers

An alternative to tube artillery is represented by multiple rocket launchers or MRLs, traditionally a comparatively cheap, crude but effective way of bringing down mass firepower. The Soviet Army pioneered the use of MRLs and 'Katyusha' barrages, launched from the backs of flatbed trucks, were highly effective throughout the Second World War and have been copied in many armies around the world subsequently. MRLs are ideally weapons of offence and surprise, laying down a lot of fire in a short space of time with a lot of morale bruising noise and blast but they take a comparatively long time to reload. After a long period of spurning multiple rocket launchers at last the West has caught up with a system which is anything but crude, or indeed inexpensive, but which will represent a highly significant component of the US and European NATO armies' inventory for a long time to come.

Development began at the beginning of the 1970s under the title General Support Rocket System in an attempt to break the Soviet monopoly of this type of weapon while engineering in a typically American high technology advantage. It was designed around a tactically mobile and reasonably well-armoured launch platform that could keep up with tanks. A crew with minimal training should be able to fire a punishing 12-rocket broadside and reload very rapidly while automated systems and precision guidance would do the rest. In 1979 Britain, France and Germany signed a Memorandum of Understanding to adopt the system (now renamed Multiple Launch Rocket System or MLRS) as NATO standard, Italy joining in 1982 while Vought, competing against Boeing, was selected as the prime contractor in 1980. Mounted on a tracked self-propelled launcher loader (SPLL) derived from the chassis of the M2 Bradley IFV, the MLRS can fire up to 12 230 mm rockets to ranges beyond 30 kilometres. The four-metre long rockets are launched from two self-contained six-round pods, either singly or in ripple fire that takes less than a minute to complete.

The rockets themselves are unguided but that does not mean MLRS is not in the forefront of the new battlefield technology. Precision guidance begins with the launch platform itself – the launcher box trains and elevates on the bed of the SPLL under the control of the gunner who has a computerised fire-control system which can communicate with the battery computer system (BCS) or Tacfire battlefield fire-control systems (see later) and perform all the necessary ballistic communications, the re-aiming of rockets during ripple fire and loading and unloading operations. Two remote fire-control units allow operations to be carried out with the crew outside the vehicle while a new position-determining system gives the battery its own inertial guidance, telling it exactly where it is at any position without the need for surveying. The master fire-control panel has a 256-character alphanumeric display which communicates with

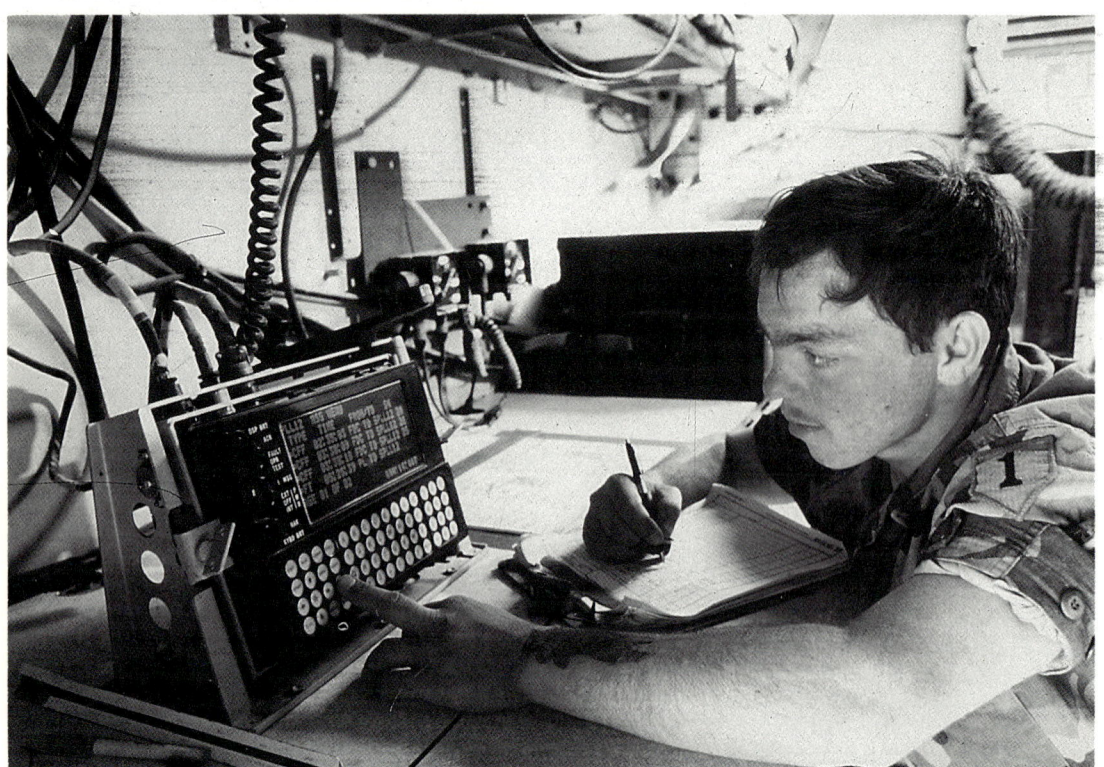

Left: Multiple Launch Rocket System (MLRS) computer control station. MLRS was originally designed to fire unguided rockets but in 1985 it was chosen as the ground launch system for the Joint Tactical Missile (JTACMS) shown right carrying smart terminally-guided submunitions. The attack footprints of Skeet and TGSMs are shown below in comparison with a 0·1 kt tactical nuclear and a one kiloton enhanced radiation weapon

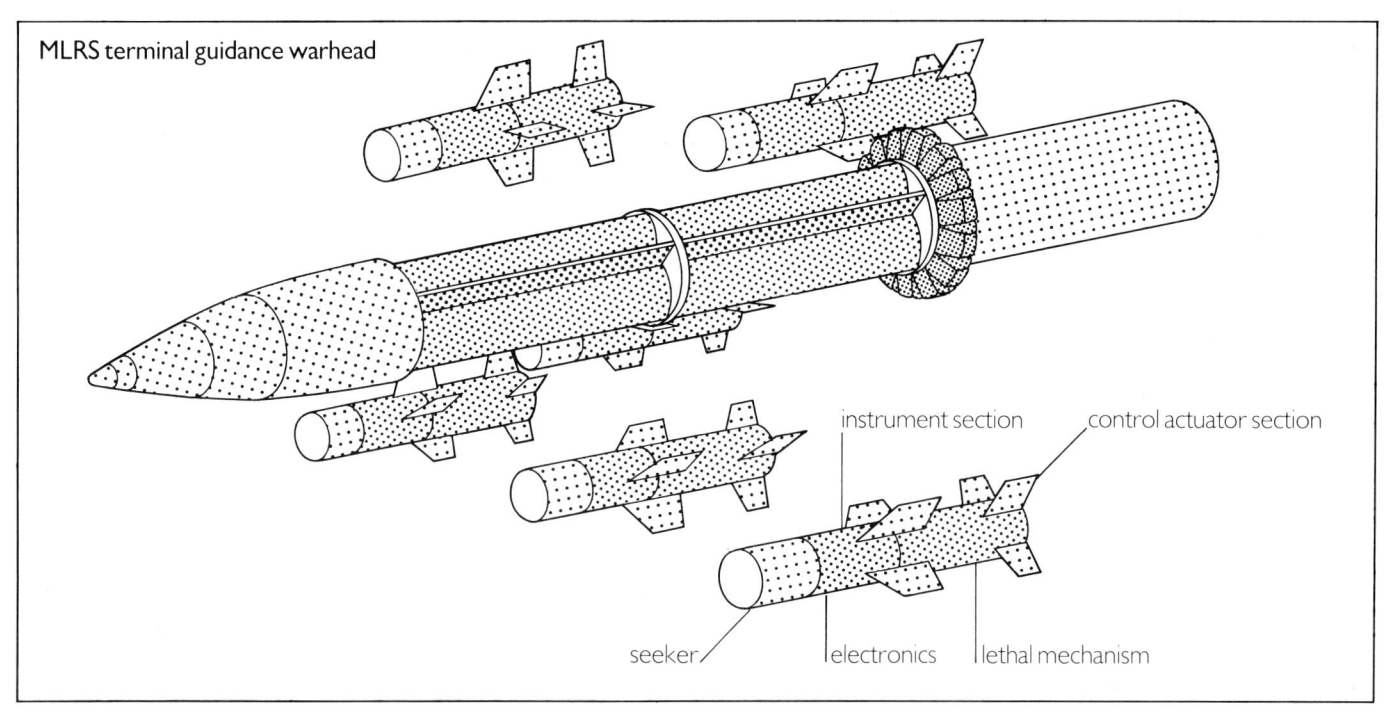

MLRS terminal guidance warhead

instrument section · control actuator section

seeker · electronics · lethal mechanism

Comparison with low yield nuclear weapons

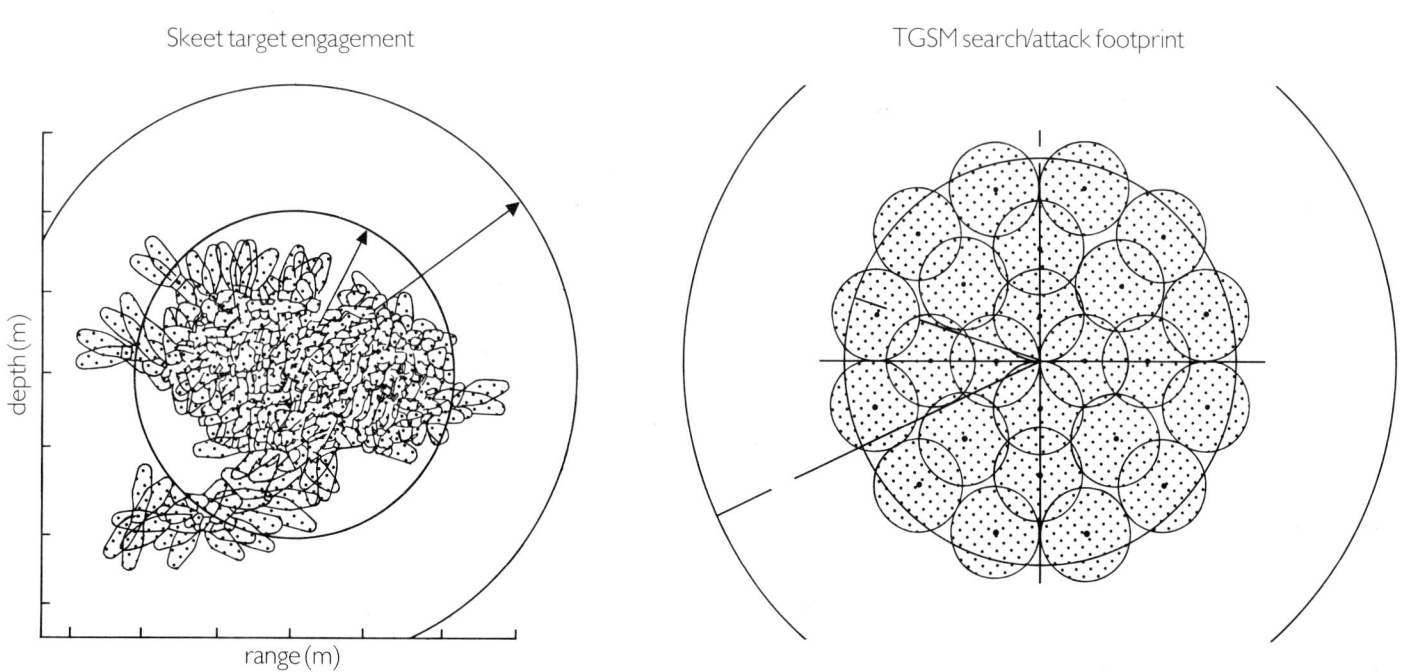

Skeet target engagement

depth (m)

range (m)

TGSM search/attack footprint

MLRS launch sequence. A full load of twelve rockets can deliver 8000 M77 submunitions creating a storm of metal and high explosive inside an area equivalent to a football pitch

the operator in plain language rather than code, or indeed in foreign languages, giving simple next move prompts. The free flight rockets are thus highly accurate but equally are designed to spread their destructive effects over a wide area. The first operational systems are designed to carry M77 submunitions each of which has destructive power greater than a hand grenade with a shaped charge enabling it to penetrate light armour. A full load of 12 rockets could deliver no less than 8000 M77s, chewing up anything inside an area of about 30 000 square yards in a storm of metal and high explosive.

This formidable destructive power is considered sufficient to destroy an enemy artillery battery. It could also be used to neutralise air defence sites within range and provide a so-called 'surge' capability to supplement conventional artillery presented with too many targets. The development of guided anti-tank submunitions will enable MLRS units to engage heavy armour in follow on formations while West Germany is engineering its MLRS batteries to dispense scatterable anti-tank mines.

Fire-control and Target Acquisition

With the US Army's original SOTAS and Battlefield Data System subborned into the Joint Stars long-range target acquisition programme, the technology for target acquisition within the remaining 'short-range' envelope still presents a formidable challenge given that the extreme

range of the US Army's new generation artillery and systems such as the MLRS is around 30 kilometres. As electronic surveillance systems multiply the number of targets that may be engaged with certainty, problems of command, control and communications expand in parallel but once again, battlefield computers are there to handle the number-crunching load. The US Army's existing Tacfire artillery fire-control was a first-generation system, the result of a prolonged and tortuous development process begun in 1967 which met Congressional suspicion once it began entering service because of apparent obsolescence – nevertheless it equips US artillery batteries at division and brigade level. Tacfire combines computing and communications in the classic marriage of information technology. A forward observer's request for fire support, for example, can be processed by the system's central AN/GYK-12 computer and mission data sent to the battalion fire officer for interpretation and forwarding to the appropriate battery. The computer meanwhile keeps stock of ammunition and processes target and meterological intelligence. At division level the system can handle tasks for up to 100 fire units including naval gunfire and tactical air operations combining up to 30 of these in a single fire plan while simultaneously storing information on 1364 targets. There are drawbacks – Tacfire lacks a secure, reliable high-frequency communications net and has been limited to line-of-sight VHF radios while data transmission diffi-

culties have made the system's processing speed irrelevant – delays simply creep in elsewhere.

The follow on system is called BCS or Battery Computer System which integrates with Tacfire but replaces voice communications with digital data links. A forward observer can transmit target information either directly to the battalion Tacfire or direct to a battery computer unit located at field artillery level. There the observer's input is displayed together with the status of the battery's individual weapons. The fire-control officer will select a gun for the mission and transmit the relevant data to the gun's own display unit.

One of the factors making computerised fire-control so important is the fact that, in contrast to past wars when indirect fire artillery had to just strike out in the general direction of the enemy, emerging electronic target acquisition methods dramatically increase the number of targets that can be engaged in real time – that is they are reported just as the surveillance system encounters them. The remotely-piloted vehicle (RPV) is an expression of this trend, an unmanned aircraft which is designed to venture into harm's way with the lowest possible 'signatures' and thus be able to survive where no manned aircraft could and, not only electronically scan areas of interest and transmit the results,

but designate targets for 'smart' indirect-fire weapons such as the Copperhead artillery shell.

The US Army's RPV programme is based on the Lockheed Aquila, originally flown as a technology demonstration programme in the early 1980s, now with a target initial operational capability by 1988 when, on current plans, an RPV unit will be assigned to each divisional artillery organisation with further ground assets assigned to manoeuvre brigades and the divisional artillery itself. Aquila looks like a miniature delta aircraft which is just what it is, driven by a ducted pusher propeller with an airframe made of Kevlar. The RPV is launched from the back of a flatbed truck and can operate for three hours at speeds of up to 180 km/h, communicating in real time via a secure data link with its controllers. The payload consists of a gimballed tv camera or a forward-looking infra-red (FLIR) target tracker and laser designator/rangefinder in a stabilised mounting, all controlled by an onboard micro-processor. What Aquila 'sees' is transmitted to the systems operations centre where the mission commander, air vehicle operator and mission payload operator watch their monitors and control the RPV's flight. The payload operator can point and zoom the tv camera or operate the ranging and target designation laser. With a target sighted, the co-

The British Barmine system (shown here towed by an FV432 APC) can lay mines at up to 600 an hour to create barrier areas very rapidly. The Ranger system mounted on top of the vehicle simultaneously strews anti-personnel mines either side of the vehicle

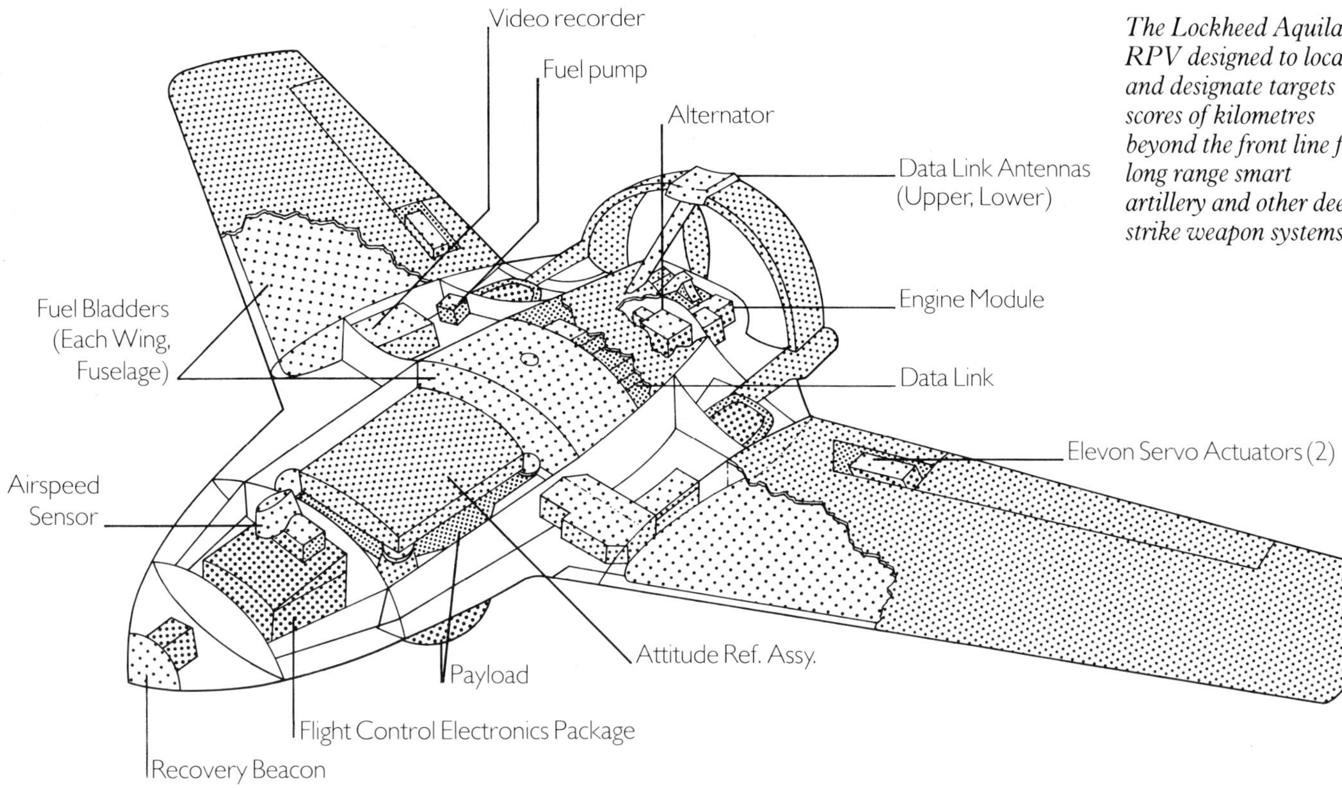

Video recorder

Fuel pump

Alternator

Data Link Antennas
(Upper, Lower)

Engine Module

Data Link

Elevon Servo Actuators (2)

Fuel Bladders
(Each Wing,
Fuselage)

Airspeed
Sensor

Attitude Ref. Assy.

Payload

Flight Control Electronics Package

Recovery Beacon

The Lockheed Aquila RPV designed to locate and designate targets scores of kilometres beyond the front line for long range smart artillery and other deep strike weapon systems

Right: The ruggedised terminal of the French CIMSA computerised battery fire-control system

Below: US Battery Computer System (BCS) field terminal. BCS can control up to twelve artillery pieces with three concurrent targets

Below right: REMBASS field monitor set

ordinates can either be computed and transmitted to artillery batteries or the designator will illuminate the target for LGBs or CLGPs. The operator can select an auto-tracking mode which keeps the stabilised camera and laser boresighted on the target regardless of the air vehicle's movement, or it can be locked onto selected targets that can be emphasised for recognition by the Aquila's own computer by the controller using a light pen on his display console. Aquila will be very important used in conjunction with the multiple launch rocket system while follow-on technology might see RPVs acting as weapons systems themselves. Stand-off weapon dispensers being developed for use on tactical aircraft might be adapted to launch from RPVs, imparted perhaps with their own degree of artificial intelligence. Such systems would be cheaper and more expendable than manned aircraft yet without the inflexibility or finality of ballistic missiles.

While the Aquila RPV provides a prying eye in the sky, the US Army has something else up its sleeve, designed not so much to 'see deep' as to tell tales. The system is called REMBASS, Remote Monitored Battlefield Sensor System which is just that, a series of sensor mechanisms which once activated can respond to noise, vibration, heat and changes in the magnetic field and interpret the results – the presence of personnel, wheeled or tracked vehicles for example. The raw data is transmitted by a VHF data link either directly or via repeaters up to a distance of 100 kilometres. As already tested REMBASS is a stay-behind system designed to be hand emplaced by the ground surveillance companies of divisional military intelligence companies – however development is concentrating on stand-off deployment by aircraft, tube or rocket artillery over areas of interest deep behind the front line. The system could then be used to cue RPV missions to provide real time images of critical enemy activity with all the automated fire-control systems waiting to bring down devastating and highly accurate firepower.

Tactical fusion – *Data handling on the battlefield*

The battlefield of the future will be awash with information – sensors, surveillance and target acquisition devices generating vast amounts of data, relevant and irrelevant, capable of potentially swamping a human command structure with an unmanageable flood of data. The solution lies once again in electronics, and the US armed forces are giving high priority to developing systems which could ease the otherwise intolerable burden on the intelligence officer and commander of sorting vital information from the less than critical. A key expression is 'Tactical Fusion' which means the process by which incoming information is collected, combined, correlated and dispensed to the relevant user. Without such a process and without its technology staying in step with deep target acquisition and deep attack systems, the whole business of striking deep would buckle up under its self generated weight of information.

The status of the various US Army and Air Force battlefield data handling projects is summarised below –

Data handling

BETA In early 1982 there were two BETA (battlefield exploitation and target acquisition) testbed installations undergoing trials at sites in the USA. These testbeds were created to explore techniques that would overcome difficulties encountered in the earlier attempts at large-scale management of battlefield tactical and related information in such programmes as the tactical operations system (TOS) which was denied funding by Congress in 1980 because of its shortcomings.

The BETA operator terminal incorporates two cathode ray tube displays, on the left an alphanumeric tabular display and on the right an eight-colour unit for map and other diagrammatic information presentation. The BETA programme is most likely to be the basis of the Joint Tactical Fusion Programme which itself is planned to lead to the implementation of a US Army All-Source Analysis System (ASAS) and an Enemy Situation Correlation Element (ESCE) for the USAF.

BETA-LOCE By 1983 BETA had been deployed with US Forces in NATO in Europe, as the Joint Tactical Fusion – Limited Operational Capability Europe (JTF-LOCE), using a computer system developed by the TRW company under US Department of Defense direction. Two more testbed installations for demonstration and evaluation of ASAS (see below) data correlation were also deployed at USAF and Army sites in the USA. In Europe the LOCE deployment consists of a central automated data processing centre, interface units at sensor ground stations, and local/remote user display terminals. The system receives and correlates inputs in near real time (that is as they happen) and these inputs include Signals intelligence (Sigint), imagery intelligence, and human intelligence (Humint).

The European configuration (BETA-LOCE) employs computer software architecture designed to detect, identify and locate target and significant battlefield threat activities by the simultaneous processing of numerous sensor reports through 'self-correlation, cross-

correlation and aggregation'. Aggregation is the computer aided process of identification of parent units based on known data concerning subordinate units based on a very large data base. So called 'future queries' allow the operator to define logical associations which will automatically initiate the cutting in of the relevant 'template' (see p114) which will aid substantially in predicting the enemy's next action. In exercises carried out in Europe during 1983 using the system, analysts were able to predict battlefield events significantly earlier than was previously possible with existing means.

JTF The Joint Tactical Fusion (JTF) system is intended to be the follow on from BETA-LOCE, a full scale system designed to provide automated facilities to process, analyse and distribute intelligence reports obtained from a wide range of sources. A longer term more advanced version is planned that will permit access to direct real-time intelligence.

ADDS The US Army Data Distribution System (ADDS) is under development as a secure, jam-resistant digital communications system that will be used to transmit data among command and control, intelligence, air defence, fire support, electronic warfare and other computer systems.

AFATDS The Advanced Field Artillery Tactical Data System (AFATDS) is described as a new generation automated fire-control system, a development programme which may prove to be a successor to the Tacfire system designed to increase the efficiency and targeting capacity of artillery batteries.

LFATDS Lightweight Artillery Tactical Data System (LFATDS) planned to be tested by the 'high tech testbed' US Army 9th Infantry Division. The LFATDS is reported to offer 'all the capabilities of the Tacfire system, but by using the latest hardware and more modern software, the system is much lighter while providing faster, simpler secure operation'.

MCS The Manoeuvre Control System (MCS) is a command and control system being developed by the US Army to provide an automated information network to assist battle staffs in operational control of the mobile units under their command. Development began in September 1980 with the introduction in the European theatre of a prototype system using microprocessors and minicomputers. The eventual system 'will consist of a network of small computers that will enable tactical commanders to have access to information on the status and disposition of their forces and those of their opponent'.

ASAS/SEWS ASAS/SEWS (all sources analysis system/ SIGINT electronic warfare sub-systems) is another US Army command, control, communications and intelligence system designed to collect and evaluate battlefield data obtained from forward observers, aircraft, foot patrols and intelligence networks. Development began in the second half of 1979.

Below: AN/TPQ-36 weapon locating radar tracks incoming projectiles and calculates the firing point, a typical information generating system for the new automated battlefield

Target acquisition

PLSS The precision/location strike system (PLSS) is being developed to provide a round the clock, all-weather capability for USAF aircraft to attack a variety of ground targets. In particular it is intended for tactical use against air defence systems that depend on very accurate guidance and detection radars to control anti-aircraft artillery and surface-to-air missiles. It uses specialised distance measuring equipment and other equipment on highly instrumented aircraft to detect electronic emissions from enemy radars and relay that information to a ground-based central facility. The computers there analyse the data, comparing inputs from multiple aircraft to pinpoint the type and location of a radar. This information is then available for use in mounting a strike against the radar. Using photogrammatic techniques, a form of aerial reconnaissance photography, PLSS will also be able to establish the locations of targets that emit no electronic radiations.

Joint STARS Joint Surveillance and Target Attack Radar System (Joint STARS) is a combined US Army/USAF development programme formed by the merging of USAF's Pave Mover project with the Army's Battlefield Data System (BDS), which, in turn, supplanted SOTAS. The Joint STARS radar system is foreseen as a key enabler of deep strike warfare able to locate and track moving targets at extended ranges in any land battle of the year 2000 and beyond. It will give target position information for indirect artillery fire and use of other weapons such as the projected Joint Tactical Missiles System (JTACMS) with target ranges extending more than 100 kilometres into hostile territory.

Airborne tests of a multimode surveillance radar (MSR) proposed by the Boeing/General Electric team competing in the JSTARS programme have already demonstrated detection and location of moving targets on the ground in real-time. Each sweep of the radar cumulatively adds new detections to the display and in this way high traffic areas can be detected and additional intelligence data derived from it.

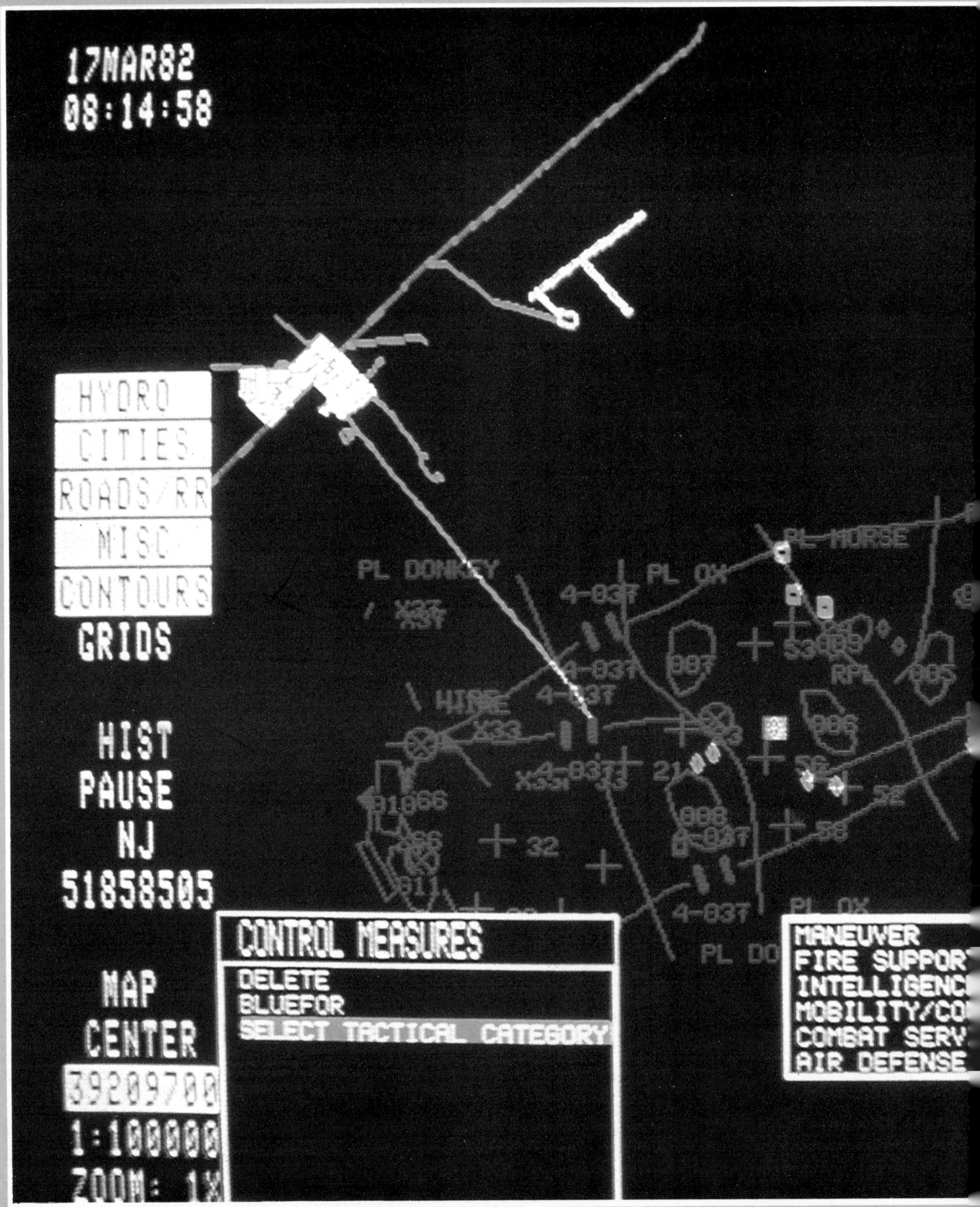
17MAR82
08:14:58
HYDRO
CITIES
ROADS/RR
MISC
CONTOURS
GRIDS
HIST
PAUSE
NJ
51858505
MAP
CENTER
39209700
1:100000
ZOOM: 1X
PL DONKEY
PL OX
PL MORSE
CONTROL MEASURES
DELETE
BLUEFOR
SELECT TACTICAL CATEGORY
MANEUVER

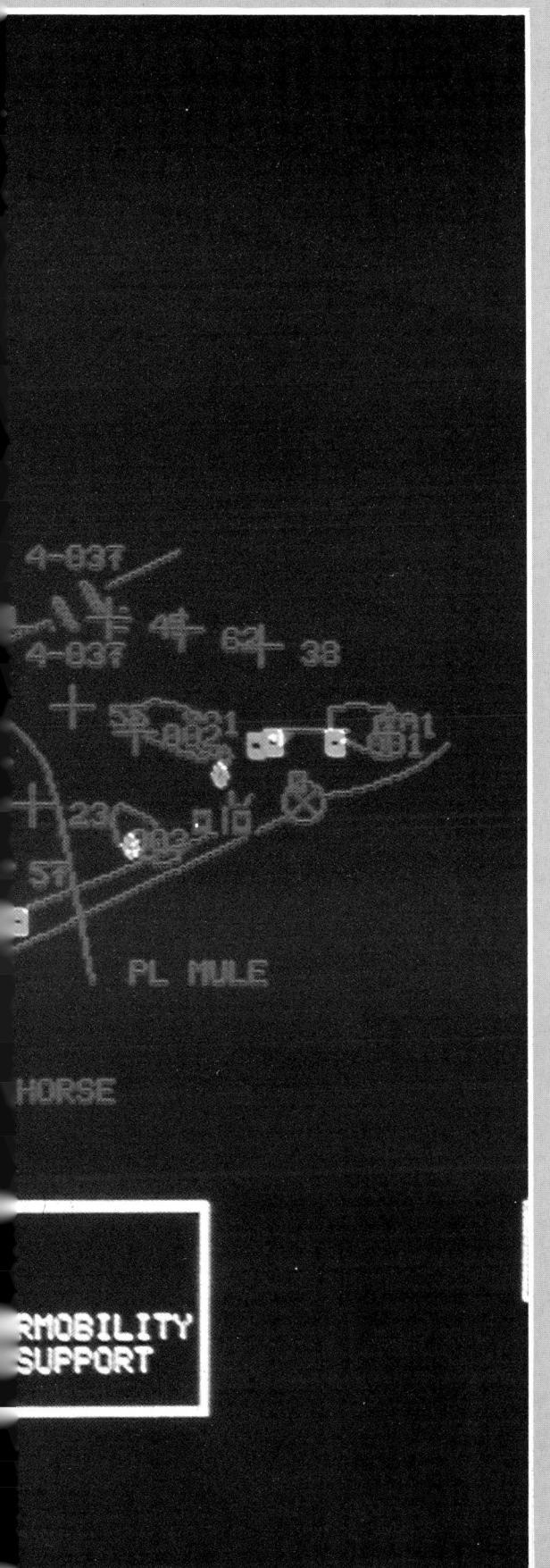

STRIKE SHALLOW:
Alternatives to AirLand Battle

'The choice between an offense-dominated world and a defense-dominated world is, in the end, the fateful choice that lies before mankind.'

Freeman Dyson, *Weapons and Hope*, 1984

4

The idea of deep strike, whether expressed as Follow On Formation Attack or as AirLand Battle, has been attacked on military grounds with questions concerning its actual efficacy and relevance, and politically with questions concerning whether it does anything to enhance deterrence and to scale down the risks of a nuclear war in Europe should deterrence break down.

The military questioning begins with the perception inherent in both doctrines of the Soviet way of war – the rigidity of its command and control structure and in the principle of echeloning. The contradictory thesis is that changes underway in Soviet doctrine mean that devoting attention to the all conquering follow on forces is a fundamental mistake. The real target should be holding the lead strategic echelon, the nineteen Category I divisions making up the group of Soviet Forces in East Germany. This hinges on assertions by several highly regarded analysts of Soviet force structure that rigid echelonment, working to strict timetables is a thing of the past – that a fast paced and administratively competent Soviet Army could concentrate forces on a broad front with light screening forces probing for weaknesses, to be exploited as and when found. This would be the job of independent Operational Manoeuvre Groups (see Chapter 5) driving for deep objectives without any 'second operational echelon'. The influential British Soviet-watcher Christopher Donnelly wrote in 1983, 'If the offensive is in one operational echelon, NATO's plans for interdiction ... against a second operational echelon [reinforcements for the western military districts] will be in vain. There may well be no such second echelon within East Germany for several days.' SACEUR countered this contention robustly (claiming along the way that SHAPE took account of external views such as Donnelly's as long as they matched intelligence inputs; the Sandhurst view apparently agreed with FOFA). General Rogers claimed that the OMG was only one option for employing follow on formations, that if an OMG did penetrate NATO's defence then it would be a priority target for counterattack using all the target acquisition and firepower of FOFA technology.

The second line of attack falls on the technology itself and the high promises made for it. While the core technologies march apace with or ahead of industrial and consumer computing and information technology, battlefield environments are a different matter. Acquisition systems that must overfly hostile air defence are vulnerable (although less so than manned aircraft) and their data links susceptible to electronic warfare. 'What is to stop a moving target indicator deep surveillance system being spoofed

and the system overloaded, by having suitably spaced soldiers with corner reflectors on their headgear running from copse to copse so as to show up as innumerable vehicles moving from hide to hide', asked one sceptic. He also proposed that terminally guided submunitions could be spoofed in similar ways, by trucks masquerading as tanks, by decoys and chaff long used in air and naval warfare, by extended exhaust pipes to distance heat sources, even by buildings and trees. In 1984 a Swedish arms

manufacturer demonstrated a giant can of foam which would quickly turn a tank into a shapeless blob and mask its heat signature – could it really be as simple as that?

Increasing onboard discriminatory intelligence may be the answer but even if technological fixes can keep target acquisition systems ahead – what to do with the data they generate? The airland battlefield can only function with access to information and enormous quantities of it – are there not limits to the system's com-

Continued concentration on small teams of infantry, highly mobile and equipped with short range but high technology weapons, is advocated by those military analysts who have doubts about the actual operational effectiveness of deep strike wonder weapons. Left is a French infantry platoon armed with Milan. The Wasp missile (above) for example, designed so that a single strike aircraft could wipe out an armoured formation without overflying the target, was cancelled in 1984 because of spiralling cost and complexity

plexity and rigidity? The section of FM 100-5 which deals with intelligence distinguishes it from 'combat information' which is 'raw data that can be used for fire and manoeuvre without interpretation or integration with other data'. Once validated, integrated, compared and analysed, raw data may become intelligence. The intelligence becomes useful once compared with so called templates which are either models based on what is known about enemy tactical doctrine, 'situational' showing what might happen when doctrinal templates are applied to a specific piece of terrain under specific weather conditions, and 'event templates' representing a 'sequential projection of events that relate to space and time on the battlefield, indicating the enemy's ability to adopt a particular course of action. Once event templates have identified the enemy's general activities, the commander and the intelligence officer direct their attention toward specific areas or windows of interest. Comparing these windows with doctrinal templates, the commander can determine the enemy's options and possible courses of action.' The same sceptic who saw funny hats as the answer to MTI radar also pounced on this last admission that

the enemy might not obey the rules with the accusation that here was an 'Achilles heel in the highly automated command and control set up: it is an invitation to the opponent to engage in deceptive and unanticipated behaviour, either outright spoofing or conduct outside the bounds of the predictable'.

These are doubts about detail expressed largely from within the military/strategic studies establishment. There are similar doubts from within and without as to the whole political and military efficacy of 'deep strike'. A repeated criticism is that the costs of deep strike systems rise as a function of their range and deep strike systems will soak up economic resources denuding close combat forces of the power to stop the first echelon in its tracks. Better to have ten robust and reliable anti-tank missiles in the hand now, runs the argument, than two high tech replacements in five years' time. And it is not just weapons systems – it is war reserve stocks, boots, blankets and *manpower* which is at risk making more perilous a situation where NATO at present simply lacks the manpower to provide for both front line forces and an operational reserve.

Right: Self propelled guns of the Bundeswehr, *the West German Army on manoeuvres*

Robotic defences

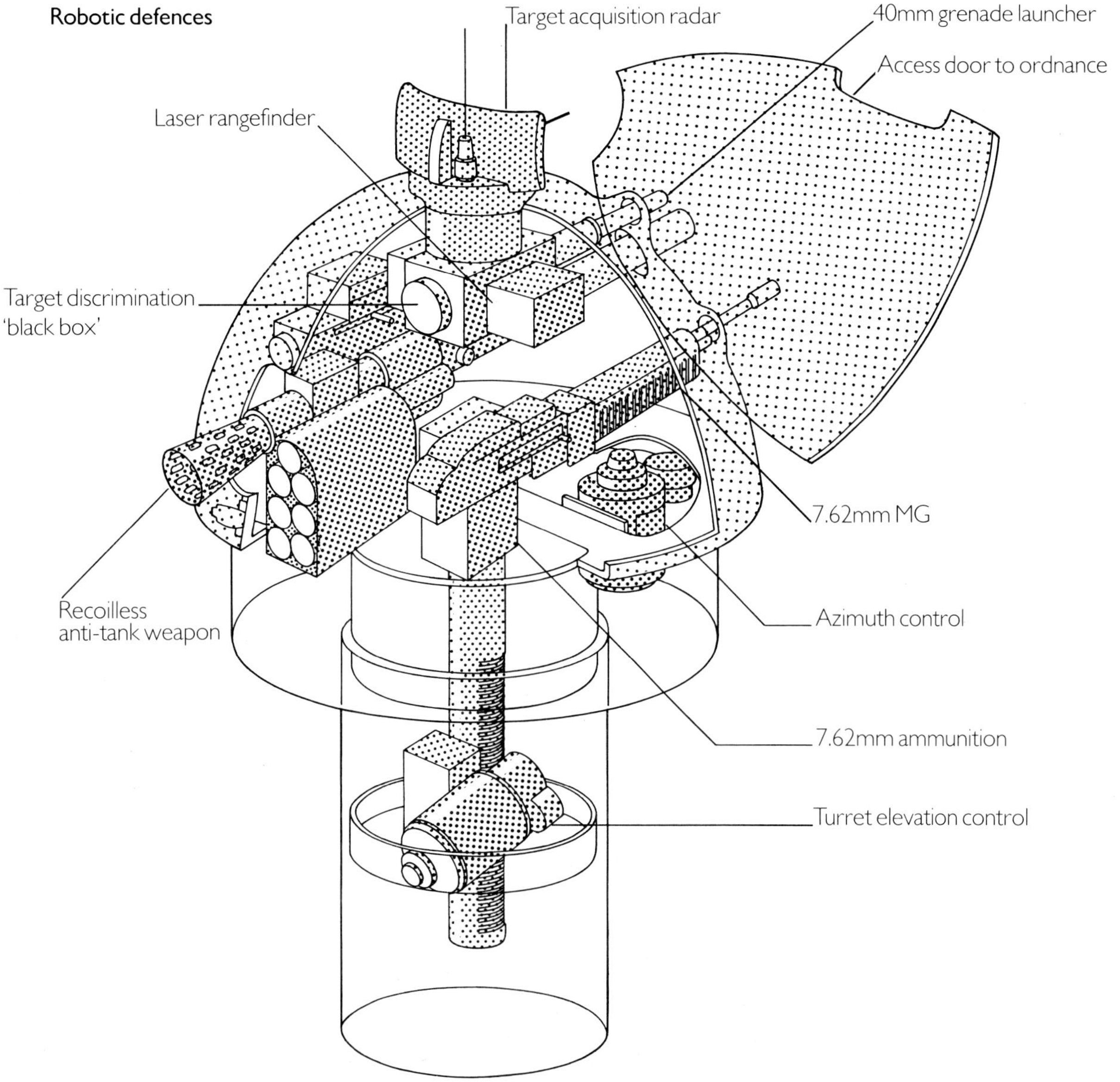

Target acquisition radar

40mm grenade launcher

Access door to ordnance

Laser rangefinder

Target discrimination 'black box'

7.62mm MG

Recoilless anti-tank weapon

Azimuth control

7.62mm ammunition

Turret elevation control

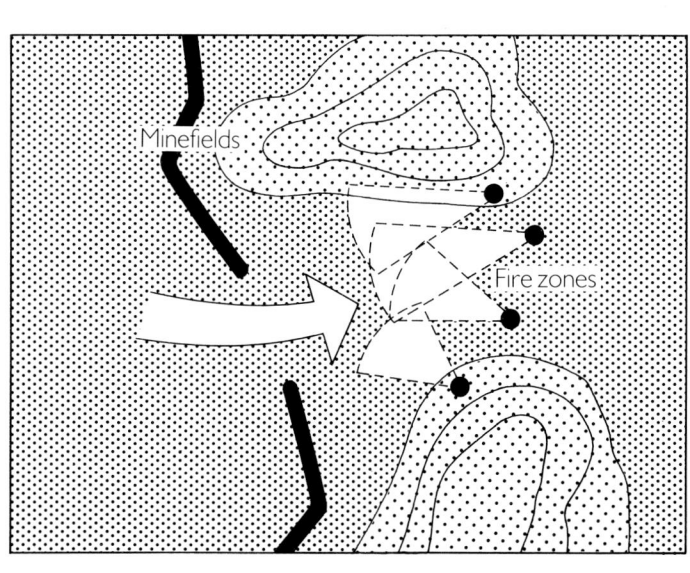

Minefields

Fire zones

One of the problems of those who advocate applying high technology to the front line battle rather than deep strike weapons is that there are strong echoes of discarded defensive doctrines of the past. The 'Maginot mentality' label is easily applied to those who argue for such solutions as barrier defences (smart minefields, 'instant' anti-tank ditches provided by pumped liquid explosive and so on). This proposal for a robotic anti-tank gun, emplaced to sweep killing zones flanked by minefields has strong overtones of the fortified lines of 1935–40 which the panzers simply drove round once they had found a gap

Left: The US Army naturally takes the opposition very seriously, seriously enough in fact to have units trained with Soviet tactics and weapons (passed on largely from Israel). This is not a still from the film Red Dawn *but a real live GI/Ivan complete with AK-47 and BMP infantry fighting vehicle*

Below: Bundeswehr *Leopard 2 tanks on manoeuvres*

Above: More than any other factor, the 1979 theatre nuclear force modernisation decision which brought US Army Pershing II rockets and USAF ground-launched cruise missiles to Europe re-kindled anti-nuclear, anti-American and anti-NATO sentiments

All the doctrines and proposals for enhanced conventional defence so far mentioned plus their detailed criticisms also assume that tactical and theatre nuclear forces continue to play a role in NATO's deterrent posture. The emphasis behind Follow On Formation Attack is that the nuclear threshold is too low but it is still there. Enhanced conventional defences are essential meanwhile because the credibility of deliberate escalation is eroding as the Soviet Union matches or outstrips the Western alliance at every level of nuclear force structure. AirLand Battle assumes that deterrence will be enhanced by conventional forces having a potential beyond mere passive defence, they can win battles at the operational level but if necessary they will do so by the use of nuclear weapons, if politically sanctioned. There are even suggestions that warfighting offensive conventional forces can enhance deterrence by threatening retaliation themselves – such as embarking on a deep counter-offensive into Eastern Europe. Or, if this sounds too fantastic and dangerous, by providing a kind of escalation option within the conventional level, to force an aggressor to desist from his aggression by holding the prospect over his head of 'losing' in a military sense, of holding under threat that which in this analysis the Soviet leadership values most, the Soviet Army, before either destroying it in detail as the Wehrmacht came close to doing in 1941, or resorting to weapons of mass destruction.

These suggestions have done little or nothing to answer those in the Western alliance who question whether the peoples of the northern hemisphere will survive long enough for a new world order, at last free of the prospect of mutual mass extermination, to emerge. As the military utility of tactical nuclear weapons has declined so have their political enemies increased – those, who may believe in deterrence at a strategic level, but who see battlefield nukes as a self-made booby trap waiting to trigger the cataclysm. Why not use the new technology to forge a shield which is both a real defence and a deterrent at the conventional level, runs the argument, strip out the notions of deep strike and deep battle and go for a high technology version of active defence with rejuvenated 'new lethality' ready to wear the Soviet juggernaut down. Several such 'non-provocative' defence proposals have been made with disengagement zones, nuclear free zones and non aggression pacts following in their wake. They call in various mixes for more territorial and reserve manpower linked to 'people's war' philosophies, and 'small is beautiful' use of high technology concentrating on advanced sensor systems with small highly mobile teams of infantry operating in assigned killing zones armed with short-range but smart missiles. To quote from one such study. 'A defence zone in Central Europe, some 50 kilometres deep would be prepared along the East-West border which is 1000 kilometres in length. This defence zone would be started with all kinds of sensors, a network of underground glass fibre cables and numerous fortified positions for troops to take cover. There would be surveillance, for example by remotely piloted vehicles and reconnaissance satellites. Highly mobile squads would be trained in the area and become familiar with it.' And from another proposal, in answer to the accusation that non-provocative, non-nuclear defence would encourage a Soviet attack, 'some objectors say that although the scheme may raise the nuclear threshold, it would lower the conflict threshold. It is indeed true that the Soviets would not risk an immediate loss of territory. They would, however, risk the loss of a substantial part of their army and air force'.

The peace movement in Europe does not subscribe to Airland Battle or FOFA even if it could understand the arcane mysteries of raising nuclear thresholds by striking deep. The military establishment, with some notable exceptions, is also loath to embrace the ideas of the non-provokers. When the author reported some of the European proposals to US Army officers at TRADOC, he was answered with an improvised blackboard diagram – an ostrich with its head in the sand.

THE SOVIET WAY OF WAR

'The Russian colossus exercised a spell on Europe. On the chessboard of military planning Russia's size and weight of numbers represented the largest piece.'

Barbara Tuchman, *August 1914*

The focus of Soviet military attention has always been on Europe, both for its own sake as the place where invaders have so consistently arisen, then during the Cold War as a hostage to its new transatlantic superpower rival.

From the 1950s onwards the stakes were raised because Europe became the launch pad for American nuclear systems, bombers and intermediate-range missiles, aimed at the heart of Soviet power. In the beginning the only way to hold Europe hostage was to keep a massive army in the field, also essential to keep less than fraternal satellites in line. Then in the Kruschev era the Soviets responded in kind to NATO's nuclearisation by deploying their own nuclear-armed bombers and intermediate-range missiles, not yet capable of mauling the United States but still holding Europe in thrall now by nuclear means. This has been a long and continuing process begun with the deployment of the SS-4 missile in 1959 (the attempt to bring the United States in range from Cuba in 1962 was made with these missiles) and culminating in the deployment of multiple-warhead, mobile and highly accurate SS-20 from 1976 onwards.

Nuclearisation of the armed forces allowed the Kruschev leadership to go boldly for its own version of the 'new look'. In a speech to the Supreme Soviet made in January 1960 Kruschev announced intended manpower cuts from 3·6 to 2·4 million and an emphasis on nuclear fire-power rather than manpower. It did not last long. The promised hydra-headed forests of long-range ballistic missiles with which the Americans would be made to 'tremble in their boots' simply were not there and strategic Soviet inferiority was rubbed in by the Cuba climb-down.

The Brezhnev regime reversed the process by putting enormous efforts into the creation of a vast strategic nuclear capability *and* ever boosting conventional forces on the ground and in the air while adding a global intervention capability in the shape of a mighty navy and long-range airlift. The armed forces of the Soviet Union grew from 3·4 million in 1964 to 4·4 million in 1980. Ground forces grew from a low of 136 to over 170 divisions while output of first division weapons systems rose to meet them. Ground forces, which had ceased to be a separate command in 1964, regained their independence in 1967 as part of the re-emphasising of conventional forces. The military service law of October 1967 which reduced the length of conscript service and lowered call-up age but introduced compulsory pre-conscription training had mixed success in increasing the Soviet Army's technical competence but overall, from the mid '60s onwards, the Soviet Army began a transformation from a balanced offensive/defensive

force into one geared to fast-paced offensive operations in minimal mobilisation times. Battlefield mobility was transformed by the introduction of new infantry fighting vehicles, airborne forces, tactical transport aircraft and large fleets of helicopters. The first BMP mechanised infantry fighting vehicles were introduced into the motor rifle divisions in 1967, a very significant tactical system which had no equivalent integrated in NATO armies for a long time (apart from the West German Marder introduced in 1972), and new generation T-64 and T-72 tanks, the technical equivalent if not superior of their NATO counterparts, began to appear in front line units from the early 1970s. Through the 1970s towed artillery was replaced by tracked self-propelled guns capable of keeping up with armoured spearheads.

The fearsome experiences of 1941–45 still lie at the heart of the Soviet national and military consciousness. Junior officers who saw that war from the cupola of a T-34 or the cockpit of a Shturmovik reached high command in the 1960s and started a massive build up of conventional forces, heavily influenced by their wartime experiences. Above: The time of crisis – a Soviet infantry unit near Smolensk a month after the German invasion. Millions were taken prisoner or killed in the opening moves of Operation Barbarossa. Left: Fighting back – Ilyushin Il-2 Shturmovik ground attack aircraft on the Stalingrad front

Tactical nuclear and chemical weapon capabilities were transformed with the introduction of nuclear-capable artillery and SS-21 and SS-23 battlefield support missiles progressively replacing the relatively crude and inaccurate twenty-year old FROGs, and liquid-fuelled Scuds and Scaleboards.

Battlefield support missiles, multiple rocket launchers and artillery shells were also liberally supplied with chemical warheads, estimated at one-twentieth of the total ammunition stockpile. The Chemical Troops of the Soviet Army, variously estimated to number from 80 000 to 100 000 provide very thorough NBC defence and training throughout the Army, the individual Soviet soldier having a high level of personal protective equipment with access from company level to special decontamination equipment. From the late 1960s onwards, Frontal Aviation, the largest component of the Soviet Air Force tasked with winning the air war above any land battle, began a transformation from a basically fair-weather defensive screen of fighters into a deep ranging, nuclear-armed offensive instrument with the introduction through the seventies of modern combat aircraft such as the Sukhoi Su-17 *Fitter* C, the MiG 23 *Flogger* B and the Su 24 *Fencer*. Soviet technologists looked at the Viet Nam War and saw the potential of the armed helicopter going far beyond the counter-insurgency lash ups of the time. The Mil design bureau began development around 1967 of a high performance assault helicopter, capable of carrying a large weapon load and a squad of troops into the battle and surviving at the heart of a European high intensity conflict. By 1974 100 *Hind* As were in service with the 16th Tactical Air Army based in East Germany.

The foundation of Soviet combat doctrine is 'Combined Arms Warfare' employing various weapons (including nuclear and chemical), bringing them together in the most effective manner to the maximum advantage. The largest field formation in wartime is the 'front', roughly equivalent to a Western army group. The Front Commander controls co-ordinated ground, air, missile, air defence and, if necessary, naval formations to carry out missions and reach objectives delineated by the General Staff. There is no fixed organisation for a Front and composition would depend on role but, in general, it would comprise two or three combined arms armies, two tank armies and a tactical air army. Airborne forces could be allotted for a specific operation while lavish provision would be made for long-range air defence, assault engineers, rocket and tube artillery, intelligence, NBC defence, signals, electronic warfare, medical, technical and logistic support.

A combined arms army would contain three

Right: Polish infantry in action with a BRDM-2 armoured car. The Polish Army contributes five armoured, eight motor rifle and one airborne division to Warsaw Pact forces

motor rifle divisions and a tank division backed up by abundant tube artillery, multiple rocket launchers and battlefield support missiles plus its own integral air defence and signals, NBC, electronic warfare, helicopter and logistic support formations. The tank army could contain three or four tank divisions and one motor rifle division with the same kind of broad based combat and service support as the combined arms army.

There are three categories of Soviet Division. Category I has complete equipment and three-quarters manpower. Category II divisions are fully equipped (with some older equipment) and manpower between 60 and 75 per cent. Category III are manned at levels below 33 per cent and short of some equipment although officer and NCO training cadres are maintained intact. Category II divisions are capable of mobilisation after 30 days, Category III after 90, the additional manpower being reservists mobilised from the military district within which the division is stationed.

The Motor Rifle Division

Motor rifle divisions in terms of numbers are the most important component of the Soviet Army and are more than just infantry set on tracks or wheels. A Category I motor rifle division has formidable striking power based on a four-regiment structure, three motor rifle regiments and a tank regiment. Each rifle regiment in turn contains three rifle battalions and a tank battalion. The tank battalion of a motor rifle regiment is stronger than its tank regiment equivalent, with three companies each of three platoons with four tanks per platoon. The motor rifle regiment has its own artillery, and an anti-tank battalion equipped with wire-guided anti-tank missiles. The regimental anti-aircraft battery is equipped with four ZSU-23-4 tracked multiple cannon and four SA-9 surface-to-air missile platoons (each with a quad launcher on a wheeled vehicle for this short-range, infra-red homing, surface-to-air missile).

The tank regiment of a motor rifle division contains three tank battalions of 31 tanks each plus combat and service support including a ZSU anti-aircraft battery. The combat support of the motor rifle division includes a Frog battalion with four launchers, an artillery regiment with over fifty 122 mm howitzers, a multiple rocket launcher battalion with eighteen multiple rocket launchers and an anti-tank battalion plus reconnaissance, engineer, NBC defence, signal, combat engineer and support units.

There is also an independent tank battalion available as a divisional reserve.

Tank Division

A Category I tank division numbers some 9500 men, less than the motor rifle division's 12000. It also has a 'square' four-regiment structure with three tank regiments, each with 95 tanks, and a motor rifle regiment with 30 tanks of its own and over 100 APCs. The support units of a tank division are very similar to those of a motor rifle division.

The marriage of intense firepower and high mobility was achieved as NATO's defensive thinking congealed around tactical nuclear weapons. The Soviets continued to emphasise conventional operations, both as a usable military tool *and* as a means of defeating the West's nuclear option by maintaining a very high rate of advance. Speed would rapidly break down the dividing lines between friend and foe on the battlefield, and conventional forces might physically overrun NATO tactical nuclear weapons before release authorisation was obtained. But how to do it in the face of a NATO defence which, nuclear weapons aside, was technologically at least certainly superior? The lessons of the 1973 war when infantry armed with anti-tank missiles proved very effective were eagerly examined and new tactics and new technological solutions were built into armoured formations to retain the primacy of the tank as the arbiter of the land battle. Tanks have always enjoyed a special place in the Soviet Army and showed few signs of falling from favour even in the nuclear age – in fact the reverse as their mass and hardness are regarded as the only viable means of operating on a nuclear battlefield, while vehicles like the BMP have given all arms the level of protection and mobility enjoyed by tank troops in the Great Patriotic War of 1941–45. Another reason, certainly, was the fact that a large proportion of the senior officers steering military doctrine in the '60s and '70s had been the young men who had seen that war from the cupola of a T-34.

Soviet military doctrine of the 1970s therefore borrowed freely from wartime experience, applying it to the problems of fighting and winning on a nuclear battlefield. The war against Germany and its numerous satellites was almost exclusively a land campaign, tactical airpower being very important, fought over enormous distances on a colossal scale. From that experience Soviet military thinking embraced an intermediate step between the tactical and strategic scale of action – that is the *operational* level implying action at Army or Front level. It is here that combined arms warfare is designed to be most self-supporting, doctrinally lucid and operationally flexible.

By 1945 the Front formation had again and again proved itself as entirely appropriate to the

Soviet paratrooper.
Tough, well trained and
well equipped, the six
Soviet airborne
divisions are configured
to strike deep into
NATO's rear areas and
survive counter-attack,
one regiment of each
division for example
being equipped with
BMD airborne
armoured assault
vehicles

Right: The Soviet T-72 main battle tank has a 125mm smooth-bore cannon firing fin-stabilised projectiles. Maximum range is over 2000 metres and the gun is stabilised to fire on the move with an auto-loader for high rate of fire. The production rate in the early 1980s was over 3000 a year

Far right: Eight-wheeled BTR-60 armoured personnel carriers still provide a substantial chunk of the Soviet motor rifle division's equipment while tank divisions use the tracked BMP for their organic infantry battalions

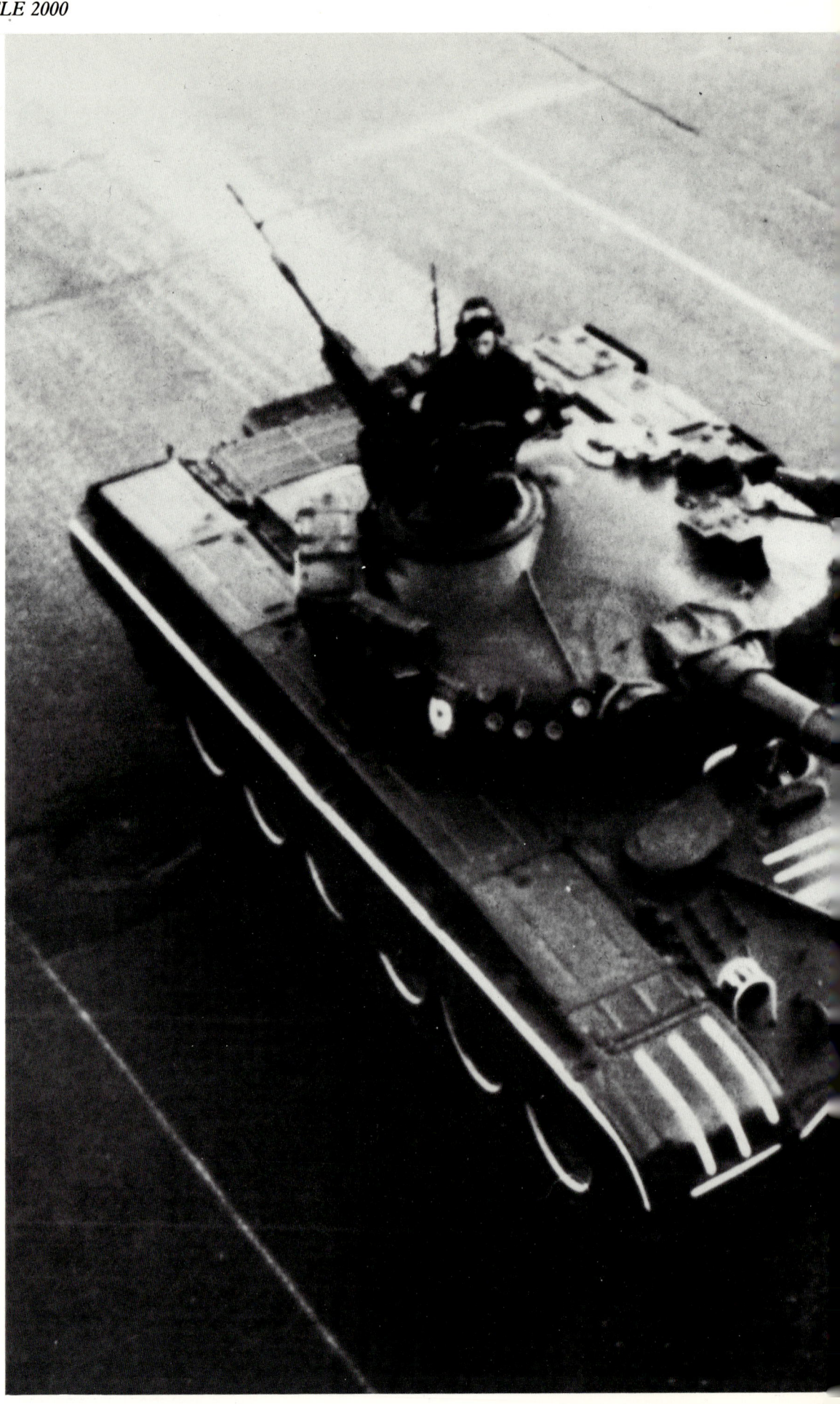

Russian soldier's way of war and as capable of confounding the Germans – yet it evolved only by hard experience after the disasters and retreats of 1941–42. The Red Army's first attempts at driving the Germans back even when made with mass armour, were largely failures. German defences were based on a shallow belt of strongpoints with excellent anti-tank firepower against which a single massive attack would founder, or, even if it broke through, would be unable to penetrate in depth and exploit. In the summer of 1942 therefore tank heavy *mobile groups* were developed to punch through in strength, drawn up as a second wave within the main attack. Here were the beginnings of a *two-echelon* formation.

The German riposte was to develop deep defences with a strong second defensive line which the mobile group could not penetrate. In turn the Red Army's Front attack was further developed into two echelons proper, the first echelon retained its mobile group and a second which could add weight to the first in the initial attack, then burn through to prise open the second line of defences for the mobile group to break through and exploit. The distinction of the second echelon from a standard reserve was that it was purpose created, ahead of time, with a defined mission.

By 1945 this double *echeloned* formation was standardised with a strong first echelon (at Front level comprising from two to seven armies) a weaker second echelon of one or two combined arms armies, a mobile group of one or two tank armies and a reserve consisting of a tank, mechanised or rifle corps. Sometimes there might even be a third echelon but equally, when the German defenders had a strong initial defence line but lacked mobile reserves with which to plug any gap, a single echelon plus mobile group would suffice. A significant study by a Western specialist in Soviet military affairs published in 1982 reached this conclusion, 'a great deal of confusion surrounds the concept of echeloning due to the unfamiliarity of the term and concept. There is no such thing as a second echelon per se. One must ask second echelon of what?... the most significant lesson to be learned from a study of development of echeloning and combat formations is that this was (a) highly variable and flexible and (b) based on a careful study of enemy defences.'

Nevertheless it became orthodoxy in Western analysis of their massive opponent that a Soviet attack would come in waves which would be echeloned both in the classic 1945 manner and designed to present a dispersed target to any tactical nuclear weapons that might detonate above the stretched out tank formations. The principle of echeloning, in these analyses, applied throughout the structure of the Soviet Army at battalion, regiment and division level and on the operational scale at Army and Front level where, according to the perceived nature of the defence, up to three waves might be deployed for the attack. But in circumstances where the defence might be surprised and rapidly overwhelmed a single wave would suffice while a small reserve would be kept uncommitted.

Facing a prepared defence requires piling up combat power on a narrower sector and the attack must be made in depth, both at Army and Front (army group) level. The relative weighting of combat power between first and second wave again depends on the nature of the defence. If a defence is offered in staged belts then the echelons will be ordered to meet each in turn, if the defence is a strong single crust, then the combat power will be vested in the first echelon the second being used to repel counter-attacks, cover the flanks, create the external front for an encirclement and replace burnt out units in the first echelon.

The level of command at which an echelon structure is adopted is very important. At TDV level (a TDV equates to a 'theatre') the 'second echelon' would be represented by forces in the western Soviet Union. At Front level, a second echelon army might be staged 150 kilometres behind the first. In the first echelon of a Front attack the component first and second divisional echelons might be staged over 120 kilometres and the divisions themselves have their regiments echeloned over distances of up to 30 kilometres.

But remember the rider that the echeloning principle was highly flexible and based on a careful study of the enemy's defences. And there are physical limits – 'formidable as it all may seem there is a limit to piling equipment on

SA-8 Gecko air defence system. The Soviet Army has made a speciality of organic air defence deploying a wide range of tactical vehicles, gun and rocket systems able to create an anti-aircraft 'umbrella' for a field formation on the move

The ASU-85 assault gun equips Soviet airborne divisions

equipment'. A single penetration by one tank army on a narrow front would make surprise almost impossible. A small fraction of its total tank strength could be brought to bear in the early moments of a battle (160 tanks) and second echelon reinforcements might take four hours to reach the original line of departure. Could this set-piece way of making war achieve the kind of momentum considered essential for non-nuclear victory?

The key borrowing from wartime experience therefore was not to be the principle of echeloning but the rediscovery of the Mobile Group, the tank heavy instrument of exploitation which had forced the pace of advance in the great battles of 1943–45. A senior Soviet soldier analysing the achievements of the wartime mobile groups wrote in 1981, 'Examples from the last war have in no way lost their relevance in theory or in practice. Rather they encourage ideas and suggest solutions to the modern problem of how to get major forces in the offensive deep into the operational depth of the defence, so as to achieve decisive aims at high speed.'

The attention of much Soviet and Warsaw Pact thinking from 1976 onwards was focused therefore on reviving the wartime mobile group concept as a means of achieving Soviet strategic goals in the case of a war in Europe by ensuring the rapid collapse of a NATO defence, the blunting of the nuclear option by very fast overrun of launch sites and nuclear weapons storage sites, and the capture of a relatively intact Western Europe. The instrument would be a modern high technology equivalent of the wartime mobile group, dubbed by Western defence analysts *'Operational Manoeuvre Group'* or 'OMG'.

Is it the Second Echelon or is it an OMG?

An OMG is a concept, not a strictly defined military unit. It could be a division, or even an entire tank army operating in support of a Front. The OMG may operate alone (but driving on objectives assigned by the Commander in Chief)

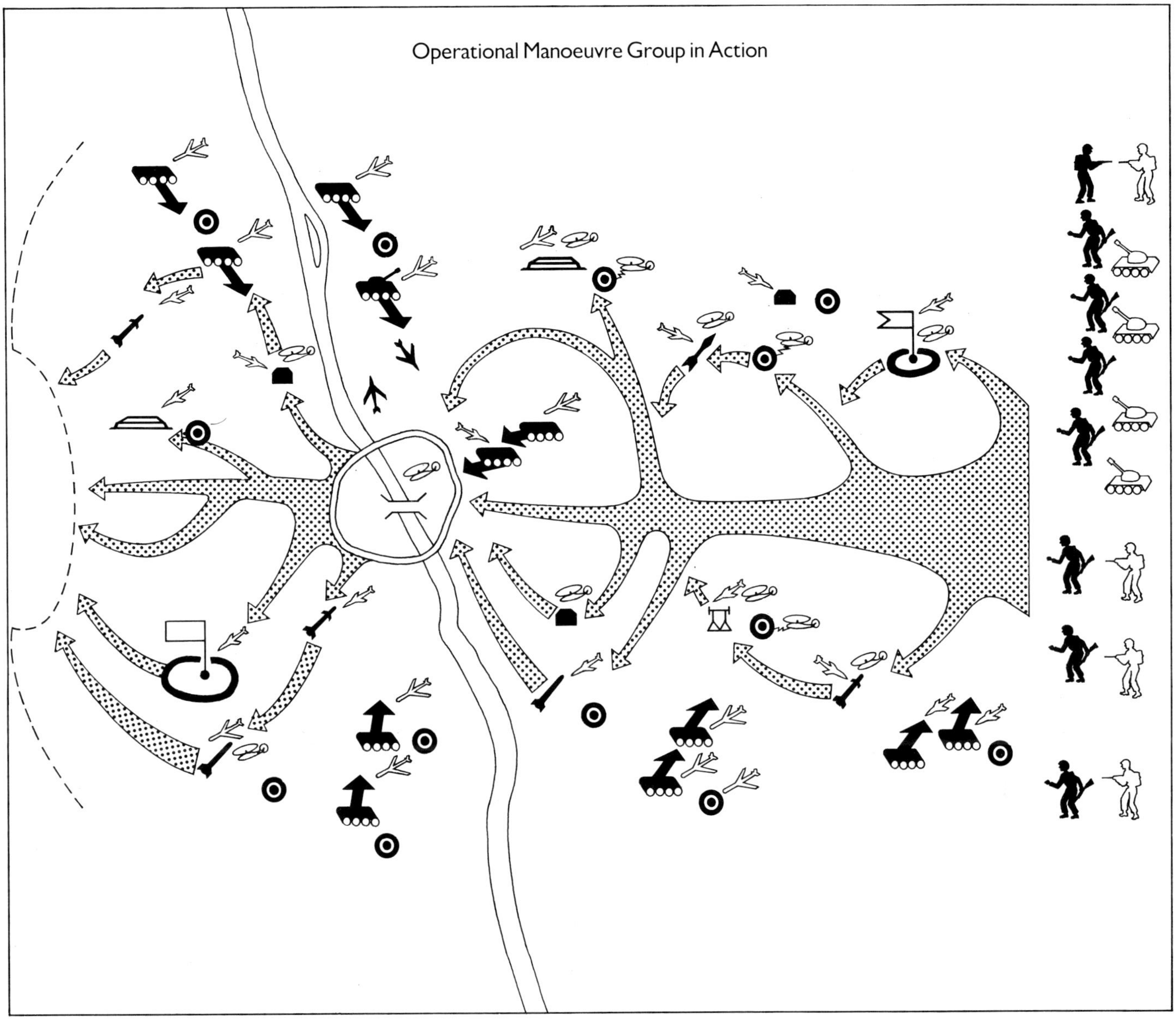

Operational Manoeuvre Group in Action

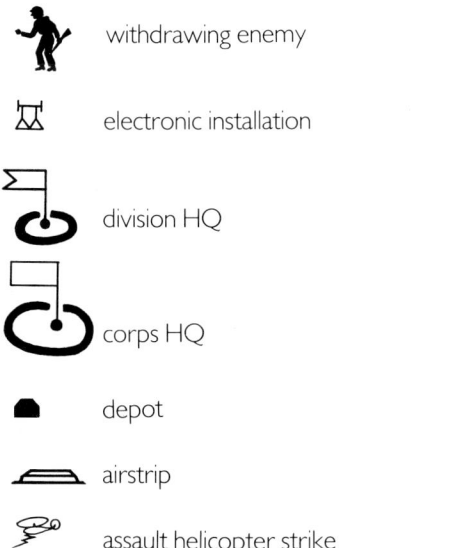

withdrawing enemy

electronic installation

division HQ

corps HQ

depot

airstrip

assault helicopter strike

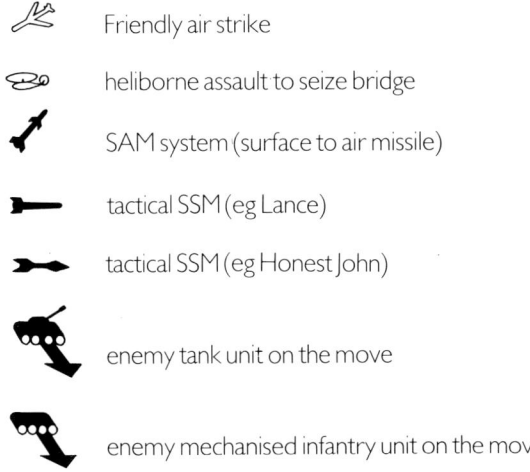

Friendly air strike

heliborne assault to seize bridge

SAM system (surface to air missile)

tactical SSM (eg Lance)

tactical SSM (eg Honest John)

enemy tank unit on the move

enemy mechanised infantry unit on the move

long-range targets under observation

or operate in concert with other OMGs with a large tactical air and rotorborne element as an essential component. It would have its fire support travelling with it in the shape of self-propelled artillery and rocket launchers. It would have its own specialists in river crossing and obstacle clearing and would be equipped for night fighting and sustained continuous operations. The OMG would also work with special purpose forces inserted in its path to seize or destroy objectives.

The threat of the OMG does more than give NATO a problem in finding reserves to shield its rear areas or putting nuclear release under even greater pressure – it compromises its own cherished plans to fight deep and return to the operational level of war (see Chapter 6). General Don Starry, commander of US Army Training and Doctrine Command (TRADOC) wrote in 1981, just as the deep battle concept was being written into US Army doctrine, 'the Corps commander is very interested in where the second echelon army of the Front is deploying. At Corps level he must tie into national target acquisition systems and other surveillance [including presumably spy satellites] to get information concerning where that army is and what it is doing. His primary responsibility in battle fighting has to do with the *follow on echelons*.'

But would they be what they seemed? A Soviet OMG riding shotgun with an Army's first echelon would look very much like its second echelon, however, in contrast to a 'typical' second echelon moving into position at a measured pace up to three days from contact, the OMG would be a self-sustaining, fast moving, firepower intensive formation geared to drive deep from the opening moves.

If a spoiling attack was launched against the OMG, NATO forces could find themselves fighting a numerically powerful opponent cut off from reinforcement or the possibility of retreat. A NATO deep attack aimed at preventing the arrival of the second echelon at Front level could equally well be bounced by a roving OMG and become engaged in a decisive battle on ground and to a plan not of its own choosing.

Furthermore, the echeloning principle has always been flexible. Without a strong NATO forward defence there may not be a second echelon in the formal sense to strike deep into. Soviet offensive assets would be piled up into the first wave, attacking on a broad front on several axes with powerful OMGs ready for insertion on each axis of advance, breaking through the second or even the first day of the offensive. NATO's plans for interdiction will be in vain as they will be striking into empty space as the real issue is decided on the front line.

FROG-7 unguided artillery rockets being prepared for firing. Range is up to 60 kilometres and warheads nuclear, chemical or conventional

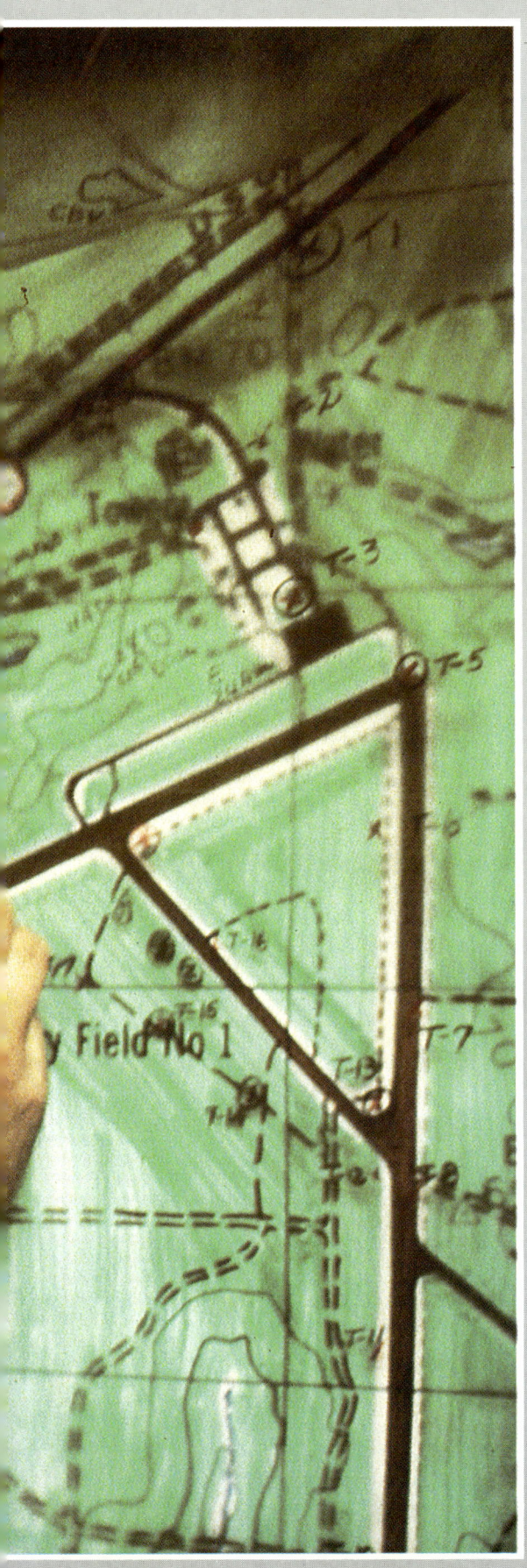

THE MAKING OF AIRLAND BATTLE

'Armies of necessity will be smaller, faster moving, depend more on manoeuvre and less on pick and shovel, though these last will still be highly important'

If War Comes by R E Dupuy and G F Eliot, 1937

From the moment when the combination of the internal combustion engine, high velocity weapons and armour plate was introduced to the land battlefield by the British in 1916, doctrines of mechanised warfare have broadly developed along two mutually opposed paths, expressed both on the grand scale in operational concepts of how to employ armoured forces and in the design emphasis of the weapons themselves. The polarity is between firepower/attrition and manoeuvre/mobility. Both combine the traditional components of warfare, fire and movement, but in a different mix.

In the doctrine that emphasises firepower and attrition, mobility is the means by which firepower is brought to bear on the enemy to cause his wearing down to defeat. In manoeuvre warfare, manoeuvre itself is the tactical, operational and strategic goal with firepower the means to crack open defences for manoeuvre to be effected – to break through, throw the enemy off balance and paralyse his ability and will to continue fighting.

US Army doctrine for a high intensity war in Europe traditionally leant to the firepower/attrition end of the spectrum. This was because

of several factors, the fact that NATO is politically and operationally configured to defend its own territory, that the political necessity of forward defence left little room for manoeuvre anyway, that NATO forces would be compelled initially to fight heavily outnumbered, and the assumption that the 'new lethality' of modern conventional weapons gave the defender an inbuilt advantage. For example, the September 1968 edition of FM 100-5, the US Army's keystone 'How to Fight' manual, described the role of manoeuvre in the offensive thus – 'In offensive operations attacking forces are manoeuvred to gain an advantage over the enemy, to close with him and destroy him' – fair enough but manoeuvre itself is scarcely emphasised as a weapon of decision.

On July 1 1976 the US Army issued a new version of Field Manual 100-5, Operations, which was again heavily underwritten by the constraints of forward defence and by an air of pessimism engendered both by the size of the Soviet war machine facing central Europe and by the army's own traumas in South East Asia. Tactical nuclear warfare was separated by a distinct firebreak which would mark in effect

The MI Abrams tank is fast, well protected, well armed and dripping with sophisticated electronics. It could certainly drive deep and hit hard but some say it is too sophisticated, and by definition too expensive, for its own good

that the conventional war had been 'lost'. The role of tactical nuclear operations was defensive – to 'negate the enemy's offensive advantage and deny him his objectives' with committed enemy units as the primary targets. Chapter 1 ended with the less than inspiring call to arms, 'The US Army must be convinced it will win'.

The 1976 edition of FM 100-5, as it said itself, set out to 'present principles for accomplishing the Army's primary mission – winning the land battle', in effect by being prepared to fight a short, intense war, 'the outcome of which may be dictated by the results of the initial combat'. The general tenor of the manual was underwritten by the concept of 'active defence'. This emphasised firepower and attrition over manoeuvre warfare and planned for a retrogressive rolling defence designed to avoid the overrunning and destruction of the defenders through a series of precisely choreographed withdrawals to prepared secondary defensive positions.

The manual emphasised two further principles, to 'fight outnumbered and win' and 'win the first battle'. Again these might be considered to be the result of a cool appraisal of the realities of the strategic balance in Europe, but the authors took comfort in the 'new lethality' of 1970s weaponry, the kind of tank slaying stopping power that had been demonstrated in the October 1973 Middle East war, the lessons of which were being equally closely studied by Soviet weapons technologists and military doctrine makers. The new lethality of such systems as infantry-portable, guided anti-tank weapons had, it was argued, greatly strengthened the capability of the defence who should be able to defeat attackers as long as 'they are never outnumbered or outgunned by more than 3:1 at the point and time of decision'. Here the tone became anything but pessimistic – TOW anti-tank gunners were told to expect first-round hits nine out of ten times at 3000 metres while 'swiftly massed field artillery, totally mobile tank and mechanised infantry battalions, airmobile anti armor weapons, attack helicopters, close air support aircraft and, in some circumstances, tactical employment of nuclear weapons offer us the means to concentrate overwhelming combat power and to decisively alter force ratios when and where we choose'.

US Army combat engineers rehearse a river crossing

The general reaction afforded to the new doctrine was good with special praise for its bluntness and a recognition of an 'old truth, the primacy of the defensive.' There was however considerable and growing dissension. As the US Army's Training and Doctrine Command's own history of the debate that followed publication of the manual summarised 'The 1976 Operations Manual was one of the most controversial ever published by the US Army ... the manual asserted new and to many, disturbing assumptions about such questions as the forward shift of the fighting balance, the lack of the traditional tactical reserve, and the ease and efficacy of the active defence's tactically critical lateral moves to concentration'.

A major issue was the perception that the 1976 manual had overemphasised the defence. An influential critic of the new doctrine offered an alternative explanation, that 'fight outnumbered and win' concealed a tacit assumption that, faced with a numerically superior enemy with a doctrine emphasising both taking the initiative and the concentration of forces, 'it is highly probable that we will lose'. He traced the failure to face realities to the Army's own institutional mind-set and in particular the parroting of the 'can-do' principle. To admit the possibility of failure would not exactly enhance morale as a whole, neither would it enhance individual careers, nor persuade sceptical politicians to loosen the pursestrings to shore up a lost cause.

The idea of 'Win the First Battle', an expression meant to encapsulate the pace and destructiveness of modern war without leaving any time for the luxury of national mobilisation, also came in for a critical hammering when taken out of context. Critics pointed out that the Soviet Army was configured to fight on the principle of echeloning (see Chapter 5) and Soviet doctrine might be interpreted as expecting to lose the first battle anyway, or rather to see its first echelon worn down by attrition before the second echelon arrived to crash through the burned out defence. FM 100-5 in fact recognised this reality in its detail but TRADOC was at pains to explain that emphasising winning the first battle was 'an attempt to offset the assumption which have governed US military policy in the past, that time and material will eventually rectify any intitial disadvantage.'

'Active Defence'

In fact active defence was the means by which it was planned to win that first battle, or rather for meeting the hammer blow of the first army echelon. The old FM 100-5 prescribed action for 'Defense Main Battle Area' thus – 'the defender must reinforce rapidly and continuously until he has concentrated an adequate defensive force ... armored and mechanised elements must be set in motion toward battle positions ... Army division commanders must be prepared to concen-

One man, one rifle – snipers in wooded terrain. However 'smart' the technology, at the end of the day it is the infantryman who must advance, seize and hold ground

trate up to six or eight heavily supported manoeuvre battalions in such narrow sectors, accepting risks on the flanks'. The doctrine strived to build in defence in depth, not necessarily by mass, but by using a relatively shallow initial defence which itself would roll back in a series of 'bounding overwatch withdrawals' where defenders would withdraw under the cover of other strongpoints just before being overrun themselves. When the enemy's main thrust was identified commanders were advised to concentrate winning levels of combat power 'using reserves from the rear' and by reinforcing laterally from the flanks. Should concentration occur at the wrong place, the mission was to countermarch mobile elements immediately. Success was judged contingent in any case on sound tactical intelligence and especially 'continuous, reliable secure communications' because 'outnumbered forces cannot afford mistakes'.

This last rider perhaps above all expressed the doctrinal weakness on which the critics of active defence and FM 100-5 from both within and outside the military establishment concentrated their sceptical firepower. It was pointed out that the 'precise choreography' called for in bounding overwatch withdrawals would put intense strain on command, control, communications and intelligence systems which would simply buckle up when subjected to electronic warfare attack. The doctrine further seemed to leave the defenders wide open to less sophisticated forms of 'spoofing' by the enemy, making feints on the flanks for example to fix lateral reinforcements in place, or doing the opposite by making a strong feint at the centre, forcing the defenders to mass at the apparent point of breakthrough before crashing through the depleted flanks in the battle of encirclement. Critics further pointed out that concentrating strength forward to 'win the first battle' not only misread the intentions of the Soviet echeloning principle but, at the front line itself seemed to revert to linear defence at a higher unit level while allowing smaller units to defend 'actively' only as far as was necessary, that is in the anti-tank attrition battle.

It was further pointed out forcefully that forward defence and the positioning of the bulk of forces in the main combat area holding critical terrain for as long as possible meant that they would be highly vulnerable to a sudden resort by the attacker to chemical or nuclear weapons, creating the very 'integrated battlefield' on which the US Army was not conditioned to

US infantry dug in with an M60 machine gun. 'Foxhole strength' still counts whatever the prevailing doctrine of the time

fight. As the seventies progressed it became more and more obvious to the critics of FM 100-5, who had the results of wargames and field exercises to point to, that NATO would have to resort to tactical nuclear weapons, not just first but early to have any chance of holding the line.

Just as these criticisms were buzzing through the Army's intellectual establishment, a new commander took over at TRADOC, General Donn Starry, posted straight from a place where such ideas as 'win the first battle' took on a more immediate meaning, commanding US V Corps in West Germany. Starry had already developed doctrinal ideas of his own within V Corps analysing with his staff a large number of possible responses to a major, tank heavy Soviet thrust on their sector. The result was a somewhat mechanistic concept called 'Central Battle'. This applied a mix of carefully thought out tactics and simple number crunching to the problem with defending US units giving battle at known ranges from known positions while terrain determined the number of enemy units that could actually advance on a given front. In this so called 'battle calculus' measurable quantities such as rate of enemy advance, enemy numbers, comparative rates of fire, number of commander decisions, time taken to receive air support and so on were computed in terms of *time* into the battle while at the sharp end the number of targets to be 'serviced' (that is destroyed) could be predicted with some accuracy.

Starry brought his Central Battle theses with him to TRADOC along with another crucial concern from the experience at V Corps – the vital factor of the Warsaw Pact's follow on forces. These forces seemed to line up in a predictable pattern and according to intelligence estimates perform in space and time in a predictable way. Could the number crunching principles of Central Battle with its ideas of 'target servicing' at the front line be applied to them too? Was the technology coming on stream to make this seem possible?

To find out Starry set his development team to work in the second half of 1977, with a brief to look hard at the new technology with both its promises and its problems of operability and training and to look at least a decade into the future. The result was the so called 'Battlefield Development Plan' published in November 1978 which added the important new idea of 'force generation' within which were the seeds of the extended battlefield and the whole business of deep strike, to that of Central Battle. Critical tasks of the Central Battle were defined as 'target servicing, air defence, suppression counterfire, C3 and electronic warfare'. Those of Force Generation were 'interdiction, C3, force mobility, surveillance-fusion and reconstitution'.

Although Central Battle and Force Generation were mutually supportive, the former was the principal function at battalion and brigade levels while Force Generation functions increased at each command echelon up through Corps to theatre – It was here that NATO commanders had the responsibility to 'anticipate Central Battles and the opportunities they would provide', that is concentrating combat power at decisive times and places while frustrating the enemy's

ability to do the same thing. To do this the commander had to 'see deep' into the enemy's rear areas and attack the enemy's second echelon forces before they reached the battlefield. As TRADOC's own history describes this crucial shift in doctrine 'General Starry's aim in using the new functional framework of the Battlefield Development Plan was to get division and corps commanders away from thinking in terms of branch organisations and capabilities. Instead,

he wanted them to think in terms of the new functions and concepts which he felt had become critically important in modern battle.'

Then there was the issue of technology. The Battlefield Development plan of 1978 also forecast an environment in which technologies such as armour protection, real time data transmission, thermal imagers and command and control advances would produce as many problems as solutions but would open up the pro-

MI Abrams tanks on the move. Tracked bridgelayers accompany them to keep an armoured spearhead manoeuvring deep in hostile territory on the move

spect of fighting the deep battle with tremendous effect.

In fact the 'new lethality' by which the 1976 FM 100-5 set so much store was already the result of the first precision guidance revolution in weapons technology. The Viet Nam war (as well as providing a proving ground for the 'new lethality') had diverted financial resources from mainstream weapon system research and development programmes. Now by the late 1970s these were back in place and the first results were beginning to appear as hardware. These included the improved conventional munitions artillery programme, rapidly deployable mines, the multiple launch rocket system, the M1 Abrams main battle tank, the M2/M3 Bradley infantry fighting vehicle, the M901 improved TOW anti-tank combat vehicle, the Sergeant York division air defence gun, the Patriot air defence missile, the Stinger man-portable surface-to-air missile, the AH-64A Apache anti-tank helicopter, the UH-60A transport helicopter and a plethora of command and control systems ranging from infantry-portable laser designators via computerised artillery fire-control to deep target acquisition systems such as the Aquila RPV and SOTAS.

These new generation weapons with their tremendous firepower and reach were obviously going to be capable of far more than 'active defence' but at the same time needed a massive organisational review to integrate their sophisticated technology and make it work effectively within a flesh and blood army. An important study called Division 86 was begun in 1978 as a spin off of the Battlefield Development Plan to do just that and reassess the workings of the Army's manoeuvre, that is its mobile ground combat units.

The primary manoeuvre unit of the US Army is the division of which since 1956 there had been three types – armoured, mechanised and infantry with one airborne and one air assault division providing special capabilities. The division is the largest force that is trained to fight as a self-sustaining combined arms team capable of conducting independent operations, normally however, the division fights as part of a corps made up of between two to five divisions. The type of divisions differ in the number and type of 'manoeuvre battalions' allotted, all of which have three manoeuvre companies. Before reorganisation the breakdown was:

Armoured division: six tank battalions (54

The 1980s saw a wide range of equipment enter service with the US Army including the M2 Bradley IFV (above), designed to transport a squad of six infantrymen into battle while keeping pace with the main battle tanks (above) and the M901 Improved TOW Vehicle (left). The ITV is basically an M113AI APC with a twin TOW anti-tank missile launcher. Twelve TOWs are carried and over 1000 ITVs were deployed by 1981

tanks each) and four mechanised infantry battalions (75 AFVs each)

Mechanised infantry division: five tank battalions and five mechanised infantry battalions

Infantry division: one tank battalion, six mechanised infantry battalions and nine infantry battalions.

The thrust of Division 86 (which concentrated on the armoured and mechanised infantry formations) was to place greater emphasis on smaller tactical formations at the platoon and company level and, by using these as the building blocks, increase the ratio of 'leaders to led'. The tank platoon for example has four tanks instead of the previous five, the tank company with three platoons has 14 tanks (two in the company headquarters) instead of the previous 17 and so on. At battalion level both the tank and infantry battalions would have four manoeuvre companies instead of three. This reflected the smaller size of the companies themselves but offered the battalion commander the flexibility of a four as opposed to a three-company structure and thus the ability to commit or keep in reserve one or two companies as battle conditions demanded. Other factors guiding the reshaping of the manoeuvre battalions were that the headquarters of a tank and mechanised infantry battalion would henceforth be similar in organisation and more compatible and that companies should only operate a single major weapon system, thus simplifying the technical demands on the commander and his men. This meant therefore that mechanised infantry companies would no longer have organic mortars and anti-tank weapons. All of the M901 Improved TOW vehicles (ITVs), for example, in the Division 86 structure are organised into anti-tank companies of 12 vehicles each with one such company found in every mechanised infan-

try battalion. An ITV company was not added to the tank battalion because of space constraints while any option that traded off a fully fledged tank company for an ITV company was also rejected.

At division level the number of battalions needed to produce the same combat power in terms of tanks and infantry squads on the ground was reduced (from 11 to 10 in Europe-based divisions) which left some force structure overhead to be allotted to other parts of the division.

The Division 86 study also concentrated on the all-important logistic support organisation redesigning forward support battalions around the kind of uptake of ammunition the new intense firepower systems would require. The Soviet model of highly capable organic air defence for ground combat formations was closely studied and to some extent emulated with the development of systems such as the Sergeant York divisional air defence gun while the same is true of engineer battalions designed to be equipped with the new M9 armoured combat earthmover engineer vehicle.

It was obvious that the technology of command, control and communications was going to dominate any combat environment that the newly re-organised manoeuvre units might face but, meanwhile, organisation itself could assist the process. The importance of the Combat Electronic Warfare Intelligence (CEWI) battalion which integrates electronic warfare and intelligence planning at divisional level thus centralising control of the increasing abundance of ground based sensors and jammers under the divisional commander's control was enhanced. The target acquisition battery of the divisional artillery was also emphasised as a component of the new look division equipped with fire finding radars and, eventually with the Aquila RPV. In addition to the organic artillery brigade, Division 86 also added a combat aviation brigade at divisional level, something unique to the US Army. The combat aviation brigade has two battalions of attack helicopters, 42 aircraft, with all the flexibility and battlefield mobility unique to rotor wing aircraft.

New technology and new ideas. It was in this intellectual climate that the first shots of the real doctrinal battle were fired – the outcome of which would bury 'active defence' and replace it with a plan for making war imbued with the spirit of the offence – the AirLand battle doctrine.

AH-64A Apache attack helicopter in action firing a broadside of unguided 2·75-inch rockets

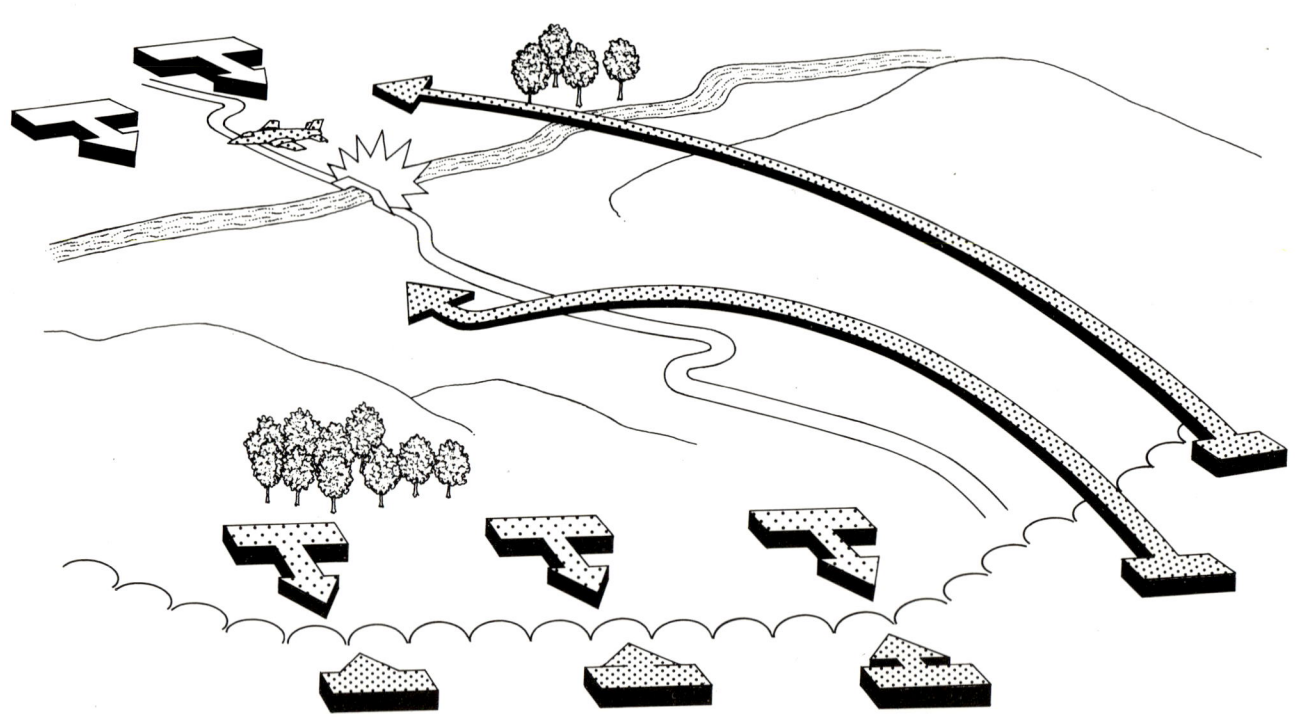

In June 1979 General Edward C Meyer, about to take up the post of Chief of Staff of the Army, suggested to General Starry that TRADOC begin to consider formal revision of the 1976 FM 100-55 both to satisfy the critics of its over passive tone and to make it more applicable to conflicts other than simply a Central Region slogging match against the Soviet juggernaut – the continued turmoil in the Middle East and Iran underlined this point. Meyer additionally thought that the manual should be enlarged in scope to embrace Corps and Theatre level battles and that the presumption of single axis break-through tactics by the Warsaw Pact was too simplistic.

The Chief of Staff's initiative could not have been better timed. TRADOC was already working hard along with the Field Artillery School and the Division 86 planners at the Combined Arms Center on the idea of second echelon interdiction, both 'seeing deep' and operating deep if necessary. As TRADOC's own history records, 'the subject of deep interdicting operations was of first order importance. It was one of the most important aspects of the whole doctrinal problem and central to the debate in which firepower, manoeuvre and the air land forces relationship all were prominent issues.'

The disintegrating superpower diplomatic climate brought about by the Soviet invasion of Afghanistan allowed at long last a realistic re-appraisal of tactical nuclear and chemical weapons on their battlefield. These 'systems program reviews' made in late 1979 and early 1980 updating the status of doctrinal, training and hardware development in the nuclear-chemical field, were the first in the post Viet Nam era.

Three very high powered meetings were held at the end of 1979 which sharply moved doctrine making towards both the extended battlefield and the 'integrated' nuclear/chemical battlefield. On 11 October 1979 TRADOC's Planning Air-Land Directorate presented the new army view of the air and land battle strongly emphasising attacks on the Soviet follow on forces to the Army and US Air Force Chiefs of Staff and the commander of the USAF Tactical Air Command General William L Creech, stressing the time factor of the arriving Soviet echelons and their perception of the sortie requirements for the necessary air interdiction. A week later this 'twenty star' Army Air Force meeting was followed by formal presentation of the Division 86 studies to General Meyer who approved the new heavy division in concept and authorised a major expansion of the studies to apply to the light

Above: 'Deep Attack' as seen by the 1982 edition of FM 100-5. While the first echelon is held at the front line, interdictor aircraft disrupt the second echelon's lines of communication. In addition defending forces drive deep to disrupt, delay and destroy the follow on forces. To quote the manual – 'If the enemy is prevented from reinforcing his committed forces, even temporarily, he may be defeated piecemeal'

Right: The Emerson Electric 'Tactical Radar Threat Generator' is designed to simulate potential hostile electronic warfare systems for realistic operational training

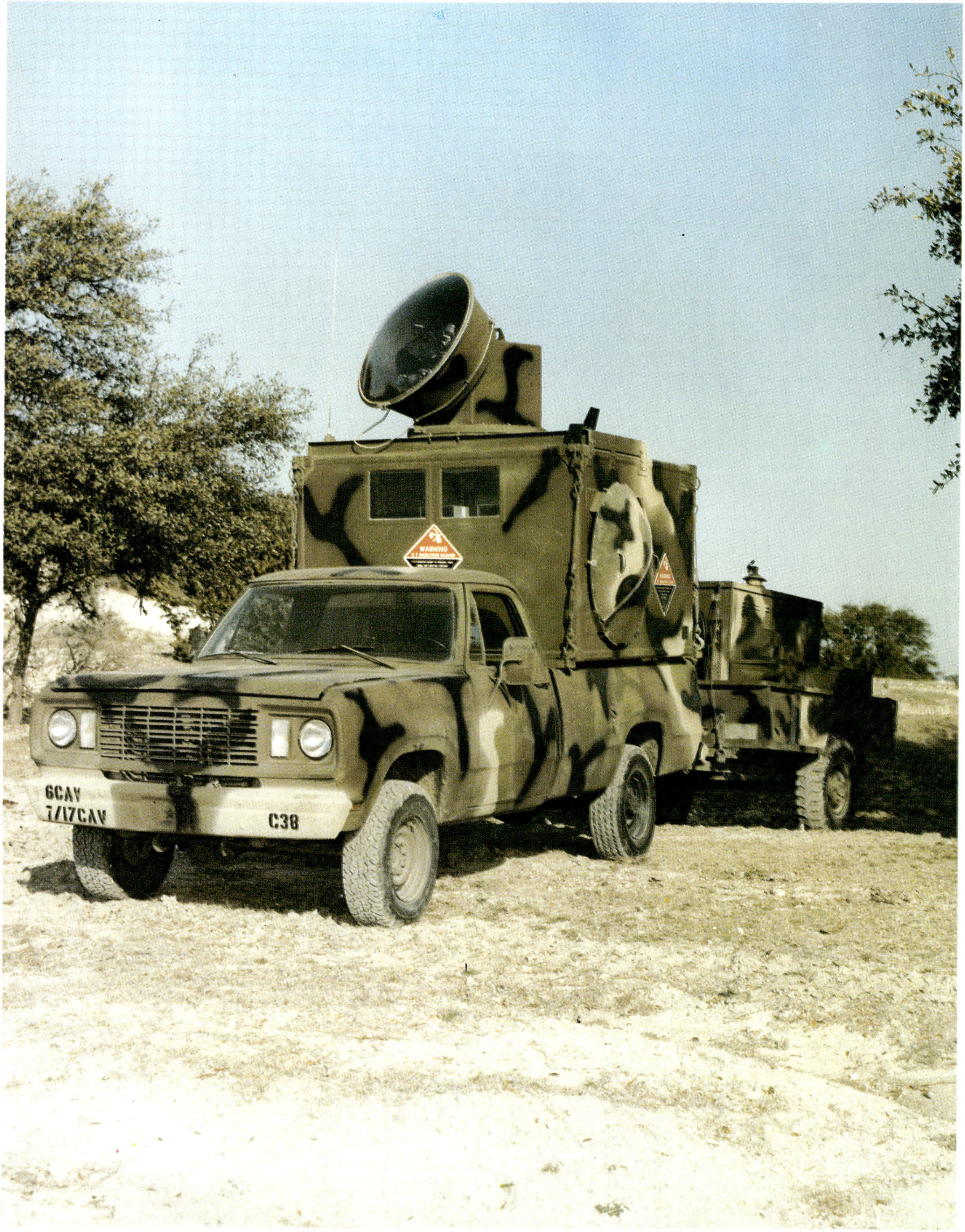
WARNING
6CAV
7/17CAV
C38

division, corps and echelons above corps – in fact the Corps 86 study had already been underway for some weeks at the Combined Arms Center at Fort Leavenworth.

A third meeting, the Nuclear System Program Review, held at Fort Sill on 18–19 December 1979 was also a very significant signpost on the way to AirLand Battle. A group of planners from the Field Artillery School, several of whom had been on General Starry's staff at V Corps, formally presented the concept of the 'integrated battlefield' which included a tactical nuclear option for deep interdiction, and the prospects for conventional interdiction enhanced in effectiveness by new technologies in target acquisition and in secure real time communications. They presented the possibility of using interdiction firepower not just as a near random response to enemy initiatives but to 'set the terms of the battle' and manage it in depth so as to 'shape the central battle, producing a configuration of enemy forces in time, space and strength adapted to their defeat.' Here it was – Central Battle and Force Generation were not separate entities, there was only one battle.

Above: M2 Bradley and M151A2 light vehicle crews take a break from manoeuvres

Right: Airborne anti-tank gunner in cold weather gear sights a TOW

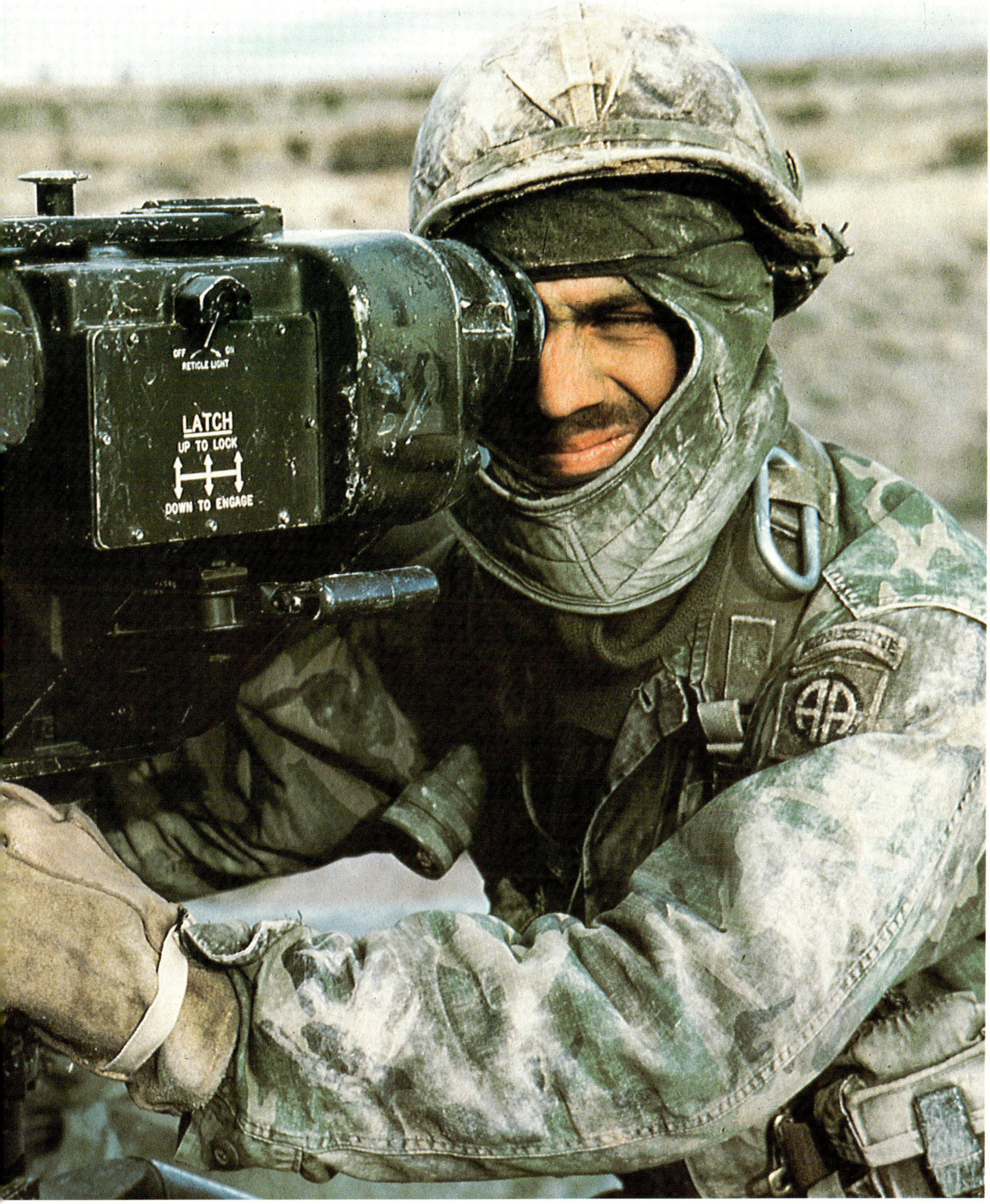
OFF ON
RETICLE LIGHT
LATCH
UP TO LOCK
DOWN TO ENGAGE

The high technology light division

It is stressed from the beginning of FM 100-5 that AirLand Battle doctrine is applicable to situations around the world wherever the US Army may find itself called upon to deter a threat or indeed to fight. The United States national experience from the Iranian hostage crisis of 1979 to the fiasco in the Lebanon in 1983, punctuated by success in Grenada plus the Reagan administration's concentration on the perceived threat of Marxist insurgency in Central America has served to lift the eyes of the military from the grey skied horizon of Central Europe to the wider world and its dangers. Thus it was of significance, but not unnatural that the first US Army division to form as a 'High Technology Test Bed' to test out and devise tactical doctrine for the prototype equipment that would come onstream for the whole army through the 'eighties should be a new 'Light Division' designed for rapid response global deployability. Such forces would exist in parallel to the Rapid Deployment Force to which the US Army already contributed the 82nd Airborne Division and the helicopter borne 101st Air Assault Division 'organized and trained primarily for rapid response and forcible entry operations worldwide.'

Right: The C-17 next generation transport aircraft is being developed to combine the short field tactical capability of the Hercules with the range and payload of the C-141B strategic airlifter to deliver rapid deployment forces straight to the scene of action

Below: C-141B arrives at Grenada. The new Light Division is configured to be airportable in 478 C-141B sorties

Below: C-130B Hercules tactical transport drops a palletised M2 Bradley in a low speed pass

In contrast the new Light Division would not have a 'forced entry' capability but would rather go into a troublespot 'by invitation' where they would be self sustaining for at least forty-eight hours. Nor would they be expected to oppose a mass tank attack but would be earmarked for use in jungle, wooded or urban terrain where they would have an advantage. They would not themselves have tanks or heavy AFVs (on paper they require half the airlift of an equivalent airborne division) but instead emphasise early arrival, seizing the initiative and operational flexibility with so called 'plugs' of extra support being called on if necessary.

Although designed in the first place for low intensity operations, the new light division might be called on to fight alongside heavy mechanised divisions on a European battlefield for example in urban situations.

The 9th Infantry Division, based at Fort Lewis, Washington State began to be recast as the first High Technology Light Division from 1982 onwards. A total of three are planned by 1990 with one found by the National Guard. The technological emphasis is on the individual infantryman and his fighting power – all are equipped with night observation devices for example and the division's 'foxhole strength', its ratio of fighting men to logistic support is higher than a standard division (3267 fighters out of 10 000 or 2·7:1 support to combat. Out of a standard division of 18 500 a mere sixteen per cent are front line combat troops). In spite of having no tanks or armoured personnel carriers, the division cannot really be considered short of firepower – over 8500 M16 rifles, 162 Dragon and 44 TOW anti-tank missiles, 54 105 mm howitzers, 36 4·2-in mortars, 18 Vulcan anti-aircraft guns and 40 Stinger SAMs plus 29 AH-1 attack helicopters. Mobility is provided by 37 UH-60 Black Hawks, 152 five-ton High Mobility Multipurpose Wheeled Vehicles ('Humvees') and no less than 694 fast attack vehicles, a kind of high powered militarised dune buggy. Men and material could be airlifted in 478 sorties by C-141B in less than four days to any point on the globe, a great improvement over the standard division which requires 1500 sorties and two weeks to perform the same task.

Below: the Emerson Electric developed Fast Attack Vehicle (FAV), a lightweight, high powered all terrain vehicle within which the high-tech light division might go to war

Above and right : US paratroopers go into action. The US Army's 82nd Airborne and 101st Air Assault Divisions are assigned to the Rapid Deployment Force trained and equipped for 'forcible entry' operations. The Light Divisions in contrast would only operate where they were 'invited in' or, in the NATO context, in mountainous or urban areas

The Integrated Battlefield

The group within the Field Artillery School had done something very significant. The operational concept advanced at the Fort Sill meeting combined the current deep strike second echelon attack ideas with tactical nuclear release and with manoeuvre operations. Major John S Doerful bluntly spelled out to the senior Army commanders assembled, the evidence of the Soviet way of war. Those follow on forces, regiments, divisions, and armies, would simply burn through a NATO defence however roughly its lead assault formations were handled. However competent the 'target servicing', firepower alone would only prolong the agony of a battle of attrition which would inevitably be lost.

Only by combining the idea of the front line battle and the interdiction of the second echelon could the circle be squared. Furthermore, in their analysis, it would only work if the ability to carry out tactical nuclear strikes was built in from the start. The prospect of nuclear strikes, even if never effected, held the enemy under risk and discouraged the enemy from massing for a breakthrough but meanwhile the existing procedure for obtaining release from the National Command Authority was too cumbersome and time consuming and materially affected the defender's conventional capability with its diversion of resources.

The answer was to assume no distinction from the start. As TRADOC's own history put it 'Doerful presented the significant implications: There was no non nuclear battlefield environment any more. By the time a commander could clearly demonstrate the time to be right for use of nuclear weapons, it would be already too late. Commanders could not afford to plan and prepare for nuclear dependent manoeuvre operations unless release was assured. Air and long-range missile systems alone might provide the only viable counterstrike capability. Integrated battle planning had to produce a decisive change in the course of the battle. The aim of fighting the integrated battle should be to win – not to avert defeat.'

In January 1980 General Starry TRADOC's commander sent the Army Chief of Staff General Meyer a report of the Nuclear Systems Program Review with an action list for change. It was warmly received and the next month General Meyer circulated a paper applauding the new developments and asserting 'we must aggressively define our nuclear and chemical doctrine ... and gain its acceptance by the national leadership and our allies'. It was clear that acceptance of the idea of the Integrated Battle, assuming as it did that US use of tactical nuclear weapons was designed to win battles not just avert defeat, plus the new emphasis on gaining

the initiative and attacking follow on forces, now required at the very least substantial revision of the Army's doctrinal training and literature. In the first half of 1980 that work began in earnest.

Corps 86

Meanwhile there was the work going on at the Combined Arms Center at Fort Leavenworth to draw on, 'Corps 86' analysing the new responsibilities of the Corps level of command, which itself would make an important input into the doctrinal melting pot. It was plainly perceived that responsibility for second echelon interdiction would fall on the corps commander, which was also the level of command at which the concerted army and air force efforts had to be coordinated. Deep strike and air-land operations were already therefore the study's principal concerns before anything else.

Left: M198 155mm howitzer. The US Army's newest towed howitzer can hurl a conventional or nuclear shell up to 24 000 metres. With rocket assisted projectiles the range is 30 000 metres. The M198 can fire conventional high explosive, submunition, illuminating and smoke rounds, binary chemical weapons or the M785 nuclear projectile with a yield of up to 5 kilotons

Below: A computer wargame simulator – a long way from the front line but a vital tool in the development of the AirLand Battle doctrine

But the results of the studies presented in May 1980 set out the Corps commander's responsibilities in a new way. Using NATO's forward defence precept as a foundation it showed the commander's view of the 'deep battle area' stretching out in time and space from the forward line of troops (FLOT) deep into enemy territory. The deep battlefield included a corps area of *influence* out to 150 km beyond the FLOT and an area of *interest* 300 km out, in terms of time for the follow on forces within those areas to arrive at the front line, up to 72 and 96 hours respectively. It was the corps commander's responsibility to see the enemy second echelon army and attack it, by tactical nuclear means if necessary and if authorised to do so, out to 72 hours beyond the FLOT. Furthermore those attacks against the enemy's first wave and follow on forces might begin immediately on the opening of hostilities.

The Extended Battlefield

Corps 86 certainly helped codify the ideas that were still hanging in mid air as the decade rolled over but it was not the whole story. In March 1980 General Starry together with his deputy General William R Richardson who was running the team at the Command and General Staff College's Department of Tactics (DTAC) based at Fort Leavenworth who would actually carry out the task, formally put in hand the revision of FM 100-5 with a directive to correct its deficiencies rather than overturn its principles – in particular incorporation of integrated battlefield concepts and its perceived overemphasis on the defence and on firepower at the expense of manoeuvre and to widen the manual's scope away from Europe.

Meanwhile as the DTAC team got down to their brief, General Starry at TRADOC was anything but intellectually exhausted and was pushing the doctrinal debate even further. In October 1980 he presented a new synthesis of the developing doctrine under the title the 'extended battlefield' which emphasised depth as much as nuclear integration and the importance of manoeuvre in opening up the battlefield allowing the US commander to seize the initiative. But it was also becoming clear that the expression 'extended battlefield' did not encapsulate accurately enough the full meaning of its evolving concepts. After discussions with General Richardson, Starry went for 'AirLand Battle', an expression designed, as TRADOC's

own history said, 'to describe the whole concept of interaction – not only that between the Air Force and the Army, but also that which occurred between all air and ground capabilities, in a firepower and manoeuvre context.'

On March 25 1981 TRADOC went public publishing Pamphlet No 525-5 on 'The AirLand Battle and Corps 86' as a concept paper for discussion and review and not as 'tablet of stone' doctrine. The AirLand battle concept was described as an approach to military operations that realised the full potential of US forces by blending the notions of extending the battlefield and the integration of nuclear, chemical, conventional and electronic attack across the full depth of an enemy's formations. Simultaneously General Starry broadened the debate by publishing an influential article in the US Army's in-house journal *Military Review* entitled 'Extending the Battlefield'.

Starry came straight to the point: 'The extended battlefield is not a new concept. It is a more descriptive term for indicating the full potential we must realize from our acquisition, targeting and weapons systems. The battlefield and the battle are extended in three ways – first the battlefield is extended in depth with engagement of enemy units not yet in contact to disrupt the enemy's timetable, complicate command and control and frustrate his plans, thus weakening his grasp on the initiative.

'Second the battle is extended forward in *time* to the point that current actions such as attack of

Left: Redeye was the US Army's standard shoulder fired, heat-seeking, surface-to-air missile, now being replaced by Stinger. Hand held SAMs give the individual soldier at the front line the chance to hit back or at least deflect strike aircraft

Right: Longer range low altitude air defence is provided by the Chaparral system, the missiles based on heat-seeking air-to-air Sidewinders

*Above: However
sophisticated the
technology and however
subtle the plans for its
use, it is no good if it
won't work under
battlefield conditions or
is beyond the grasp of
the men who must
operate and maintain it.
A tank for example is
only as effective as its
engine is reliable*

*Left: AN/TPS-43E
tactical air defence
radar foward deployed
under camouflage
netting. The system is
designed to be carried on
two M35 trucks, to be
light enough to be
tactically mobile yet
rugged enough to
withstand hard
battlefield use*

follow on echelons, logistics and manoeuvre plans are interrelated to maximize the likelihood of winning the close-in battle as time goes on.

'And lastly the range of assets figuring in the battle is extended towards more emphasis on higher level Army and sister service acquisition means and attack resources.

'What emerges is a perception of the battlefield in which the goal of collapsing the enemy's ability to fight drives us to unified employment of a wide range of systems and organizations on a battlefield which, for corps and divisions, is much deeper than that foreseen by current doctrine.'

Soon after Starry's article appeared a new version of FM 100-1, The Army, was published being the manual officially setting out the US Army's rationale, principles and force structure. General Edward C Meyer, Chief of Staff of the Army, approved the document on 14 August 1981 setting his seal on the nine 'principles of war' therein which the Army would use as a 'frame of reference for analysis of strategic and tactical issues'.

The traditional nine principles – objective, offensive, mass, economy of force, manoeuvre, unity of command, security, surprise and simplicity are considered on a strategic and at a tactical

level but it was in the discussion of the principle of the offensive 'seize, retain and exploit the initiative' that a shift from the passive doctrine of the past broke through. 'No matter what the level, strategic or tactical, the side that retains the initiative through offensive action forces the foe to react rather than act.'

Meanwhile the team at DTAC were completing the drafts of the revised FM 100-5, passing them chapter by chapter to Starry and Richardson until a co-ordinating draft, imbued throughout with the spirit of AirLand Battle was ready by January 1981. A special contact team from the Combined Arms Center was set up to spread the word and gauge reactions as the paper was 'staffed' throughout all major Army command headquarters and indeed throughout the Army as a whole, in some cases down to battalion level. By June 1981 the final draft was ready and sent to the Army Chief of Staff for approval. It was to be a year however from General Meyer's approval in August 1981 until the new FM 100-5 was finally published. One reason was the input of the new commander of TRADOC General Glenn K Otis who took over command in August 1981. Otis was particularly concerned that the US Army's 'how to fight' manual should play up the idea of the 'operational level of war'.

AirLand Battle - Fundamental Principles

Note: The following is a condensation of the precepts for AirLand Battle set out in *Field Manual FM 100-5, Operations* published by the Department of the Army, Washington DC, USA on August 20, 1982.

The Challenge

Field Manual 100-5, Operations is the authoritative statement of the US Army's combat doctrine for worldwide application. The current doctrine is called 'Airland Battle' which provides general guidelines that US Army units, primarily corps and below, would use to fight on the modern battlefield. That battlefield might be Central Europe where the enemy would be the mass mechanised armies of the Warsaw Pact, it could be southeast or northwest Asia or it might be fighting Soviet-equipped insurgents or terrorist groups in any part of the world.

Further that battlefield may no longer be characterised by distinct front lines but by rapid movement and intense volumes of fire with forward and rear areas equally vulnerable and blurring into one continuum. As the manual put it 'Airland battle doctrine takes a non-linear view of battle. It enlarges the battlefield area, stressing unified air and ground operations throughout the theatre. It distinguishes the operational level of war – the conduct of campaigns and large-unit actions – from the tactical level. It recognises nonquantifiable elements of combat power, especially manoeuvre which is as important as firepower. It acknowledges the importance of nuclear and chemical weapons and of electronic warfare, and it details their effects on operations. Most important, it emphasises the human element.'

The manual conveyed a vigorous offensive spirit from the start. As FM 100-5 puts it – 'AirLand Battle doctrine

Left: US Infantrymen wait at the treeline to go into the assault

Below: The M9 new generation 'high speed combat earthmover'

is based on securing or retaining the initiative and exercising it aggressively to defeat the enemy. Destruction of the opposing force is achieved by throwing the enemy off balance with powerful initial blows from unexpected directions and then following up rapidly to prevent his recovery . . .'

The basic tenets of AirLand Battle doctrine are initiative, depth, agility and synchronisation. *Initiative* is covered first and subordinates are exhorted to 'act independently within the context of an overall plan. They must exploit successes boldly and take advantage of unforseen opportunities . . . they will take risks, and the command must support them.'

As for *Depth* the manual prescribes that 'Commanders need to use the entire depth of the battlefield to strike the enemy and to prevent him from concentrating his firepower or manoeuvring his forces to a point of his choice.'

Agility emphasised flexible organisations and 'quick-minded, flexible leaders who can act faster than the enemy'.

Synchronisation was vital but meant more than just co-ordinated action. It meant a continuous grasp by subordinate commanders of the overall plan. 'Synchronised, violent execution is the essence of decisive combat . . . and, applies both to conventional forces and, when authorised to nuclear and chemical weapons.'

Levels of War

The new manual laid great emphasis on the operational level of war and and its place in the scope of military operations. 'War is a national undertaking which must be co-ordinated from the highest levels of policy making to the basic levels of execution. The strategic level employs the armed forces of a nation to secure the objectives of national policy. The operational level of war uses available military resources to attain strategic goals within a theatre of war. Most simply it is the theory of larger unit operations. Tactics are the specific techniques smaller units use to win battles and engagements which support operational objectives.'

Dynamics of Battle

The new manual also stressed that the dynamics of battle encompassed not only such concrete factors as firepower but intangibles such as morale, leader motivation and boldness. At its heart was 'combat power' made up of the following component elements –

Manoeuvre Manoeuvre is the dynamic element of combat, the means of concentrating forces in critical areas to gain and to use the advantages of surprise, psychological shock, position, and momentum which enable smaller forces to defeat larger ones.

Firepower Firepower proves the enabling, violent, destructive force essential to successful manoeuvre through suppressing the enemy's fire, neutralising his tactics, and destroying his ability to fight.

Protection Protection is the shielding of the fighting potential of the force so that it can be applied at the decisive time and place. It includes actions to counter the enemy's firepower and manoeuvre, such as security, dispersion, cover, camouflage, deception, suppression and mobility.

Leadership Leadership is the crucial element in combat power. The primary function of leadership is to inspire and to motivate soldiers to do difficult things in trying circumstances. The leader, as a tactician, must be able to plan his battle with an understanding of the imperative of combat.

Deep Battle

The dimensions of depth were time, resources and distance with battle in depth aiming to destroy or disrupt the enemy's forces not yet committed while cutting those already committed off from support. As the manual states 'The deep battle supports the basic scheme of manoeuvre by disrupting enemy forces in depth, that is not already in contact. If successful, it prevents the enemy from massing and creates windows of opportunity for offensive action. The corps is the primary focal point for intelligence collecting and command in the deep battle, and the primary assets for deep attack are air and artillery interdiction. Unconventional forces can also interdict enemy movements in depth, and although tactical electronic warfare systems do not have the range to affect deep targets, they can free artillery units for the deep battle.

Commanders will fight the enemy in an *area of influence* designated by the next higher level of command, and will monitor activities in its *area of interest* – where enemy units may affect future operations. The corps will strive to maintain surveillance over an area of interest large enough to give 96 hours' notice of the approach of enemy divisions and armies. Its area of influence should extend far enough beyond the FLOT to permit it to engage enemy forces which can join or support the main battle within 72 hours.'

The new manual gave even more precise definitions to a commander's areas of concern under the heading of tactical intelligence. 'In an *area of influence*, commanders locate and monitor the progress of those enemy formations that can affect their current operations, fighting them when necessary with organic and supporting means.' . . Commanders were to monitor enemy forces beyond the FLOT (forward line of own troops) or attack objectives according to these criteria.

Areas of Influence

Level of Command	Time beyond FLOT or Attack Objectives
Battalion	up to 3 hours
Brigade	up to 12 hours
Division	up to 24 hours
Corps	up to 72 hours
Army	up to 96 hours

The manual also defined areas of interest extending beyond areas of influence. They included territory occupied by enemy forces capable of affecting a commander's operations in the near future.

Areas of Interest

Level of Command	Time beyond FLOT or Attack Objectives
Battalion	*up to 12 hours*
Brigade	*up to 24 hours*
Division	*up to 72 hours*
Corps	*up to 96 hours*
Army	*beyond 96 hours*

Means to the End

Manoeuvre

The new doctrine departed substantially from that of the mid 'seventies by emphasising the importance of manoeuvre. 'US Army doctrine balances manoeuvre with firepower. The two are inseparable and complementary elements of combat . . . the co-ordinated use of both characterises all operations.'.

Fire Support

Firepower provided the destructive force essential to successful manoeuvre but could also be used independently. Commanders meanwhile 'maintain flexibility of their fire support by holding some artillery in general support, giving contingency missions to some artillery units, and reserving some allocated close air support for unforeseen circumstances.' When nuclear weapons were available, the manual allowed that 'fire support may become the principal means of destroying enemy forces. The manoeuvre may then be designed specifically to exploit the effects of fire support.'

The manual prescribed in detail the roles that various arms of service would be expected to play. 'The basic combined arms manoeuvre element of the AirLand Battle is the battalion task force, organised from infantry battalions, tank battalions and cavalry squadrons. Field and air defence artillery, engineers, air force and army aviation elements provide support. Battalion task forces can be infantry-heavy, tank-heavy, or balanced, depending on the brigade commander's plan.

'*Light Infantry* can operate effectively in most terrain and weather. In mounted operations infantry can be used to occupy strongpoints as pivots for manoeuvre; make initial penetrations for exploitation by armour and mechanised infantry; attack over approaches that are not feasible for heavy forces; capture or defend built-up areas; control restrictive routes for use by other forces; and follow and support exploiting heavy forces.

'*Mechanised Infantry* complements armour in its ability to hold ground. It provides overwatching anti-tank fire and suppresses enemy infantry and anti-tank elements. It can dismount to patrol difficult terrain; clear or emplace obstacles or mines; infiltrate or attack enemy positions; or to protect tanks in urban, wooded, or limited visibility conditions.

'*Armour* The tank is the primary offensive weapon in mounted warfare. Its firepower, protection and speed create the shock effect necessary to disrupt the enemy's operations and defeat him. Units are limited by vulnerability in close terrain, bridging requirements, and cannot climb steep grades.

'*Armoured Cavalry* is used for reconnaissance and security – to find the enemy and develop the situation – and to provide the commander with reaction time through delay.

'*Field Artillery* is the principal fire support element in fire and manoeuvre delivering conventional, nuclear or chemical fires by cannon or missile to suppress enemy direct fire forces, engage in counter-battery fires, and deploy scatterable mines. It contributes to the deep battle by disrupting enemy forces in depth and suppressing enemy air defence systems. Artillery can screen or illuminate other forces.

'*Air Defence Artillery* provides the commander with security from air attack by degrading the effectiveness of enemy ground attack, helicopter and reconnaissance aircraft.

'*Combat Engineers* perform mobility missions such as breaching minefields or building bridges, counter-mobility (building obstacles) and survivability missions.

'*Attack Helicopters* overwatch ground manoeuvre units with anti-tank fires; attack the flanks and rear of enemy formations; counter-attack enemy penetrations; conduct raids in enemy held territory; dominate key terrain by fire. Attack helicopters are even more effective when working with close air support ground attack aircraft in Joint Air Attack Teams (JAATs), but require other elements to suppress enemy air defence units.

'*Air Cavalry* performs the same missions as ground cavalry, and complements it. It can maintain surveillance over a much larger area in a shorter period of time, screen the flanks of a ground force on the move and act as a rapid reaction force.

'*Combat Support Aviation* can give dismounted and ground anti-tank units great tactical mobility, and can move towed artillery and light air defence elements or critical supplies when ground routes are blocked.

'*Electronic Warfare Units* – the military intelligence battalion (combat electronic warfare and intelligence CEWI) detects enemy communications nets and intercepts traffic for intelligence. It also directs electronic countermeasures (primarily jamming) against enemy fire direction, command/control, air defence radar, and electronic guidance systems.'

'*Special Operations* – get in depth treatment of their own. 'Special Forces conduct unconventional warfare in a theatre concentrating on strategic goals and have long-range as well as immediate effects on the battle. They include interdicting enemy lines of communications and destroying military and industrial facilities. Special Forces conduct psychological operations to demoralise the enemy and collect information in enemy rear areas.

UH-60A Black Hawk troop carrying and utility helicopters

They also train, equip and advise resistance forces in guerrilla warfare, evasion and escape, subversion and sabotage. Their greatest value to conventional force commanders is in fighting the deep battle and forcing the enemy to deploy significant numbers of combat forces to counter these activities . . . Ranger battalions are specially organised and equipped to perform reconnaissance, surveillance, target acquisition, ground interdiction and raids in the enemy rear. They can deploy rapidly to any area in the world and undertake either quick response operations or deliberate operations.'

Air Support The new doctrine categorised offensive air support as 'an integral part of fire support, delineated as battlefield air interdiction (BAI), Close Air Support (CAS) and tactical air reconnaissance, critical for identifying targets in the deep battle.' BAI was undertaken to isolate enemy forces by preventing their reinforcement and re-supply and by restricting their freedom of manoeuvre while aiming to destroy, delay or disrupt follow-on units before they can influence the close battle. Close air support meanwhile 'complements and reinforces ground fire, and may offset shortages in artillery firepower at critical times'. Also important was 'Joint suppression of enemy air defences (J-SEAD) . . . air force operations are conducted theatre-wide and in direct support of particular tactical operations such as airmobile assaults. Army surface-to-surface weapons complement these actions at campaign and local levels.'

Nuclear and Chemical Weapons

The manual came straight to the point on the use of weapons of mass destruction 'Battle planning for nuclear weapons employment involves both the unique consideration of release authority being conveyed from the National Command Authority via the operational chain of command and the use of pre-planned *packages*. A package is a group of nuclear weapons of specific yields for use in a specific area and within a limited time to support a specific tactical goal. In general, preferred targets are:
– Enemy nuclear delivery systems.
– Command and control elements.
– Support forces in the rear of committed elements.
– Follow-on or echeloned forces.
– Reserves.

'This selective targeting allows friendly forces in contact to defeat engaged enemy forces by conventional means.'
 Likewise the use of chemical weapons was politically restricted by US policy which prohibits first use of lethal or incapacitating chemical munitions. 'Only the National Command Authority can grant authority to employ chemical munitions. Commanders must be prepared to integrate chemical weapons into nuclear and conventional fire plans on receipt of chemical release.'

The Offence

The new doctrine characterised the offence as 'the decisive form of war, the commander's only means of attaining a positive goal or of completely destroying an enemy force.' Key elements of the attack were concentration, surprise, speed, flexibility and audacity. 'Surprise' allowed the commander to 'choose the time, place and means of launching his attack. This advantage must throw the enemy off balance and prevent him from recovering until the mission succeeds' while 'audacity' was the 'keystone of successful offensives'.

As for forms of manoeuvre in the attack the least preferable was frontal attack 'because it exposes the attacker to concentrated fire over the most obvious approach, frontal attack is used to overwhelm light defences, covering forces and disorganised units'. Penetration sought to break through the defence on a narrow front, widen the gap created, and seize deep objectives. It may precede an envelopment. Envelopment itself meanwhile avoided 'the enemy's main strength – his front – and produces the greatest psychological shock. It aims at gaps between enemy positions or at weak points which may be created by nuclear, chemical or conventional firepower. A turning movement is a variation of an envelopement, forcing the enemy to abandon forward positions.'

The manual characterised five main types of offensive operations – movement to contact, hasty attack, deliberate attack, exploitation and pursuit. The ideal attack should move fast and aggressively along lines of the indirect approach, following successful reconnaissance probes into areas of weakness and agilely switching strength to further prise open penetrations and reinforce success carrying the battle deep into the enemy rear.

The Defence

The new manual began by re-emphasising some well worn principles 'Defence denies success to an attacking enemy. Defensive operations are undertaken to:
– Cause an enemy attack to fail.
– Gain time.
– Concentrate forces elsewhere.
– Control essential terrain.
– Wear down enemy forces before a counter attack.
– Retain tactical, strategic or political objectives.

But new concepts in defensive doctrine were marked. Active Defense with its carefully choreographed lateral movements and bounding withdrawals was replaced by a defensive doctrine with no single technique being dominant. As the manual put it 'Army doctrine does not prescribe a single technique for defence, but allows all variations between a purely dynamic defence and a purely static one designed exclusively to retain terrain. Typically, large-unit operations combine elements of both forms: the static which controls, stops, or channels the attacker; and the dynamic which strikes and defeats the enemy's committed forces.

The key terms of AirLand Battle doctrine also apply to any successful defensive operation. They are designed to: – 'Fight the enemy throughout the depth of his formations to delay and disorganise him and create

opportunities for offensive action. The defender must organise forces and resources in depth to gain time and space for flexibility and responsive manoeuvre.
– 'Maintain agility and flexibility in using fire, manoeuvre, and electronic warfare to set the terms of battle. The defender should force countermoves on the attacker thus overloading the enemy's command and control system.
– 'Synchronise all available combat capability in co-ordinated combat actions. Violent execution of flexible plans and aggressive exploitation of enemy weaknesses can halt the attacking force.'

The deep battle in defence would also invoke the use of air interdiction, long range artillery and tactical nuclear weapons if so sanctioned, plus airmobile and special forces. Rear area protection was emphasised and commanders had to be prepared to take risks in dealing with any dangerous concentrations or breakthroughs in their own rear. Rear area threats were scaled as level 1 including the activities of terrorists, level 2, diversion and sabotage by tactical units smaller than battalions and level 3 including airborne or amphibious operations at larger than battalion size.

Meanwhile the new doctrine delineated the role of the covering force as the forward security echelon, operating 'forward of the FEBA to protect main battle area (MBA) units from surprise . . . preventing enemy medium-range artillery fire on the FEBA. The covering force gains and maintains contact, develops the situation and delays or defeats the enemy's leading forces.'

'Normally the covering force is organised around tank-heavy task forces and divisional and regimental cavalry. Ideally, a corps will employ one or more armoured cavalry regiments because they are specially organised and trained for security missions. A corps may use divisions or separate brigade units instead of cavalry or with cavalry. A light corps may have to use air cavalry, light armour or airmobile infantry in the covering force area.'

At the main battle area infantry could provide static pivots for manoeuvre if the ruggedness of the terrain allowed while armour provided the dynamic elements, 'moving between islands of resistance'. Strongpoints in contrast were static but 'located on terrain features critical to the defence or at a bottleneck created by terrain obstacles'. And once again initiative is emphasised, 'when the enemy has committed his forces, the defender tries to seize the initiative and counterattack over familiar ground protected by his own positions'.

The new doctrine was more explicit than the old on the subject of reserves. The manual writers were told to re-emphasise the importance of reserves and to play down the lateral shifting of forces that had characterised Active Defense. The manual put it thus 'the primary purpose of reserves in the defence is to counter-attack to exploit enemy weaknesses such as exposed flanks or support units, unprotected forces in depth and congestion. They also reinforce forward defensive positions, containing enemy penetrations or reacting to rear area threats. Commanders down to brigade will normally try to retain about one-third of their manoeuvre strength in reserve. Once he has committed the reserve, the commander should form other reserves from uncommitted forces or from forces in less threatened sectors.'

M60 tank equipped with a hydraulically-operated dozer blade. Combat engineers are equipped to rapidly clear obstacles in attacks and build up earthworks in defence

Reserve airmobile forces had the added benefit of very rapid response. They could be used in suitable terrain to 'reinforce positions to the front or on a flank. In a threatened sector they may be positioned in depth. Airmobile forces are also suitable for swift attack against enemy airborne units landing in the rear area . . . Because of the unique capabilities of attack helicopter units, commanders hold them in depth initially and commit them when needed, for stopping surprise tank attacks and destroying enemy tanks which have broken through defensive positions.'

Combined Operations

The manual gives guidance on operations under multinational command which are worth repeating here. 'In areas such as NATO and South Korea, the US Army will operate under procedures and principles standardised in peacetime. National combat and combat support forces are phased into NATO commands on alert of impending hostilities. National commands relinquish operational command of these forces to NATO and a similar transfer of authority occurs for post D-day augmentation forces. National commands prepare the units for combat and then transfer operational command to NATO. While the United States retains positive control of US nuclear weapons during peacetime, NATO will exercise wartime operational command of forces and delivery vehicles. NATO forces should be capable of operating effectively on the nuclear-chemical-conventional battlefield.'

Left: Improved TOW Vehicle on the move

Right: AH-1 Cobra attack helicopter pilot. Both helicopter and ITV have a primary mission of killing tanks but must engage them direct at the front line at ranges of a few kilometres with line of sight weapons

The Operational Level of War

A major criticism of active defence had been that it had simply substituted firepower for intellect and had suppressed the historic sense of the art of war, within which tactical efficiency is merely a component of the art of winning battles, what had been lost sight of was fighting at an 'operational level' midway between strategy and tactics.

The German Army had long emphasised its importance, in their great mobile defensive battles on the Eastern Front of 1943–44 they had proved its masters but in fact had written it out of their 1973 doctrinal manual – they were however in the process of writing it back and pointed this out to the US contact group in their staff review of the draft FM 100-5.

An influential article 'The Operational Art and the AirLand Battle' published in *Military Review* in May 1982, the work of the artilleryman Lt Colonel J S Doerful, succinctly defined what was meant and how this midway level of war tied in with the idea of fighting deep. The author laid out the opportunity in the Soviet Army's force structure waiting to be exploited, the vulnerability that rigid echelonment of forces and cumbersome command and control procedures laid open for an army prepared to take the offensive to disrupt and destroy with the second echelons themselves as the primary targets for deep attack. In Doerful's analysis, 'NATO deep attack units must rapidly transit the FLOT (Forward Line of Own Troops), drive deep, conduct lethal and violent attacks on the move to destroy high value elements of the uncommitted echelons as they are encountered, refuse decisive engagement, prepare for commitment to continue the attack either on the rear of the first echelon divisions or to the depth of the enemy's formations'.

Other commentators pointed out the risks involved, that operations conducted within the enemy's echelonment would mean less artillery support and would be within the enemy's air defence and electronic warfare envelope. Meanwhile the enemy himself is not going to throw away the initiative lightly – while a NATO commander might be engaging the first echelon of the enemy along the FLOT with his divisions in contact, the Corps commander while preparing to launch a deep attack with manoeuvre forces will be in effect committing his reserve, raising the risks of a breakthrough at the FLOT considerably. The deep attack force itself might be defeated in detail if it met a sizeable combined arms force in its path.

The Air Dimension

The US Air Force of course had always been in the business of deep strike and follow on forces attack, indeed before the target acquisition and precision guidance revolution the manned aircraft was the only means to carry out such attacks on mobile targets. Since 1973 TRADOC personnel had conducted regular meetings with their counterparts from Tactical Air Command at Langley AFB where a permanent Air-Land Forces Application Agency (ALFA) had been established in 1975. By the late 1970s army and air force were co-operating actively on a wide range of training projects, mission and hardware requirement analyses and by the end of the decade both commands had dipped their toes into the development of joint operational doctrine. In fact the pressure was already coming from the sharp end in Europe, from Allied Air Forces Central Europe who had already included a relatively new concept in their doctrine of offensive air support. It was called battlefield air interdiction (BAI), distinct from close air support and interdiction attacks on fixed targets and in 1979 the relevant NATO manual was ratified by the US. But the USAF was anxious to retain control of BAI missions rather than subordinate them to Army Corps commanders and said so forcefully in a position paper delivered at the end of 1979.

The stand off did not last long. Through 1980 army-air force discussions continued, a Joint Second Echelon Attack (J-SAK) study was launched and a parallel project on the Joint Suppression of Enemy Air Defences (J-SEAD) was undertaken. In May 1981 the Army and Air Staff formally reached agreement on responsibilities for the Battlefield Air Interdiction mission with a formula that gave army corps commanders the lead in locating and affording priority to targets and the air force the job of managing the means by which the mission would be carried out. There would be no doctrinal change in close air support, the attack of enemy targets in contact with friendly troops which was already the preserve of the ground commander.

These then were the pillars on which the new doctrine of the US Army was built – the principle of the offensive. The principle of taking the battle to the enemy with forces and weapons configured for deep attack (the 'extended battlefield'). The possibility of continuous warfare even after use of chemical or nuclear weapons (the 'integrated battlefield'). The principle of synchronising all available combat means, including air forces. And perhaps especially the return to the 'operational level of war' allowing and expecting US Army commanders to seize

the initiative and use it aggressively to win battles and campaigns.

These principles were synergised into the AirLand Battle concept which with the publication of the revised FM 100-5 Operations in 1982 became the official war fighting doctrine of the US Army, further agreed as the basis for joint tactical training by the US Army and Air Force Chiefs of Staff on 21 April 1983. AirLand Battle had arrived.

*A-10A anti-tank aircraft waits in a wooded hide.
Able to operate from austere forward airstrips or
even strips of roadway, the A-10 is purpose designed
for tank killing and close air support of ground
troops*

AIRLAND BATTLE 2000

'In future wars of higher intensity and shorter duration, winning will have to begin immediately. There may be only one battle . . . our initial battle plan will have to succeed.'

Airland Battle 2000, TRADOC, 1982

7

Hard on the heels of the publication of FM 100-5 enshrining AirLand Battle as official doctrine, TRADOC stirred the pot by publishing a discussion document which foresaw the kind of combat conditions the US Army would face and the resources they would require at the end of century. It was called AirLand Battle 2000 (the name was subsequently changed to Army 21) and immediately generated, along with the brisk discussion it was designed to trigger, deep confusion with the AirLand battle doctrine itself.

One was policy, the other was futurology – but the two became intermingled in a fog of obfuscation which spilled over into the parallel follow on formation attack imperatives coming from SACEUR. AirLand Battle talked of deep strike implying depths of operation up to 150 kilometres maximum behind the enemy's front line. The AirLand Battle 2000 study meanwhile almost casually talked of ranges up to *300 kilometres*, blending firepower and pugnacious, attacking manoeuvre, precisely what FOFA did not. No wonder confusion reigned.

Nevertheless as an official US Army study, Airland Battle 2000 deserves attention, dealing as it does with a not too distant time frame of 1995–2015 and thus giving more than a glimpse of the on-going pattern of doctrine making by allying many of the core precepts of AirLand Battle doctrine with new technology and potential combat environments. Further, because the weapon systems it foresees would have to be in the developmental prototype stage by the early 1990s, decisions about research and resources would have to be made through the 1980s with rival services jealously guarding their preserves.

The AirLand Battle 2000 study begins from the standpoint of the world in which US military force may find itself operating at the outset of the 21st century. Superpower bipolarity will be breaking down under the impact of industrial and economic cartels and regional blocks of nations with scarcity of natural resources threatening fundamental US interests. 'We can be held hostage for more than just oil, we are approaching a truly international economic and resource world. Dwindling US heavy production capability is no secret. Today more people work for McDonald's than US Steel' says the document bluntly.

In this world of multiple threats therefore, US forces must be prepared to operate in a wide range of terrain and conditions from Central Europe to deserts and jungles and to be able to get in quickly before threat forces can make their presence felt. Forces of the future will have to be light, self-sustaining and capable of rapid deployment. 'We must truly be prepared to win the land battle in order to be in a position to negotiate a favourable settlement. Emphasis is

on winning – we cannot afford to simply avoid defeat.'

How to win? The document projects that the US will not match any enemy in numbers but rather combat advantage will be achieved through superior weapons and C^3 systems technology. In addition wars of the future will be nasty, brutish and short. 'In future wars of higher intensity and shorter duration, winning will have to begin immediately. There may be only one battle and no opportunities to regroup after initial heavy losses. Our initial battle plan will have to succeed', say the document's authors not surprisingly.

Below: Impression of the Bell-Boeing MV-22A Osprey tilt-rotor in US Army guise. The US Army want tilt rotors for casualty evacuation and logistic support

Right: The LTV M998 'Hummer', the winner in the contest to provide the US Army with a high mobility light vehicle, bigger than a jeep but just as agile

Above: The 'Dragon', one US aerospace think tank's proposal for a vectored thrust combat vehicle for the airland battlefield of tomorrow. They say forget rotary wings and go straight to something like this

Right: Meanwhile the 'traditional' US helicopter manufacturers have their own ideas written around the LHX light attack helicopter requirement. This is Hughes' proposal for a single seat, Hind-killing air to air, air to ground combat machine for the year 2000

The document looks at the future battlefield in some detail, extrapolating operational concepts which owe a lot to AirLand Battle itself. 'The characteristics of the battlefield of the year 2000 are – large quantities of sophisticated combat systems, difficult command and control, no single weapon system will dominate, no significant qualitative advantage available, battle expanded into the airspace and into the depth of enemy formations (300 km +) with intensive battle at the decisive point.' And the study continues, 'The key ingredient of how we must fight in the year 2000 is to retain the initiative not just by traditional means but by extensive use of manoeuvre which is a blend of firepower and movement plus use of all combat assets in a truly integrated effort'.

The fundamental principles of AirLand Battle 2000 are initiative, depth, agility, time and synchronisation. Initiative means a considerable degree of decentralised decision making and ancillary studies have looked in detail at the psychology of small unit leadership and 'team spirit'. Agility is the ability to react faster and more surely than the enemy. Depth is crucial, the battlefield stretching in space by force of the greater range of weapons and reconnaissance systems, and the concentration on the enemy's forces rather than terrain as the objective. 'Enemy forces not directly engaged will have to be considered for their future influence on the battle. The threat of nuclear and chemical weapons will require dispersion of forces over greater areas ... independent and continuous actions will give depth to battle ... forces may be required to bypass or be inserted hundreds of miles apart in the enemy rear or flank positions.'

These principles are built on developments of existing doctrine made more urgent by the increase in area and depth of the battlefield and the burden of command and control being pressed into an even shorter time frame – 'everything will be faster on the battlefield in the year 2000'.

But what is really startling about AirLand Battle 2000 lies in the proposals for new kinds of military formations, the technology of weapon systems and 'bio-engineering' for the soldier of the future. First the command structure – 'We have developed four levels of command for Airland Battle 2000', reads the study. 'The Close Combat Force (CCF) is similar to what we now have in the separate brigade but with its own fire support and other organic units. The Land Battle Force (LBF) is an austere tactical command and control headquarters with no organic command or service support units. Its function is to control the close combat forces. It is very similar to our current divisional headquarters. The AirLand Battle Force (ALF) is an operational command that works within the confines of a joint or combined structure. It conducts all source intelligence, long range planning, and attacks the deep echelon of the enemy.'

Infantryman 2000

The flesh and blood soldier of the year 2000 is an example of high technology himself, just to survive in the lethal environment predicted. As the study paper says, 'Will soldiers be able to exist on the battlefield of the year 2000? Or are we imagining such a technologically hostile environment that soldiers themselves will not be accommodated? We expect in addition to more diverse physical wounds, more psychological stress casualties. Whole battle staffs of professional officers may collapse; commanders may have to be replaced or dual commands instituted. Human engineering to immunise our soldiers against stress may be required just as we now immunise against disease. Military equipment will have to take into account this aspect of human technology and conditioning. Our younger population especially is becoming more adapted to a video display and computer game environment. Weapon systems of the future must take advantage of this.'

If arcade game addicts might make good soldiers they will have a chance to try their skills with individual computer systems automatically patched into a communications net reporting their position and status. Headquarters computers would automatically update and predict unit strength as operations progressed. Spiritual comfort could be available through a two-way video link or via prerecorded, denomination of your choice, chaplains' sermons. Bio-engineered stress-reducing drugs and artificial blood plasma will tend to mind and body in more direct ways while the need to shave or relieve oneself could also be controlled by 'bodily function retarding' drugs and freeze-dried, high-energy rations.

A wounded soldier could report his position and injury via his personal communication system alerting a team of 'Mobile Medical Trauma Technicians' to come to his aid while a remote computer would already be re-routing his electronic mail and adjusting his unit's payroll. If he should die before being whisked to hospital via tilt rotor (in suspended animation if necessary) his body could be removed from the field of honour by disintegrating foam.

Below: 'Infantryman 2000', the results of a feasibility study conducted by a British research company in 1985

Above: The helmet features a built in computer system and an 'eyes-up display' flashing tactical information into the soldiers's line of sight

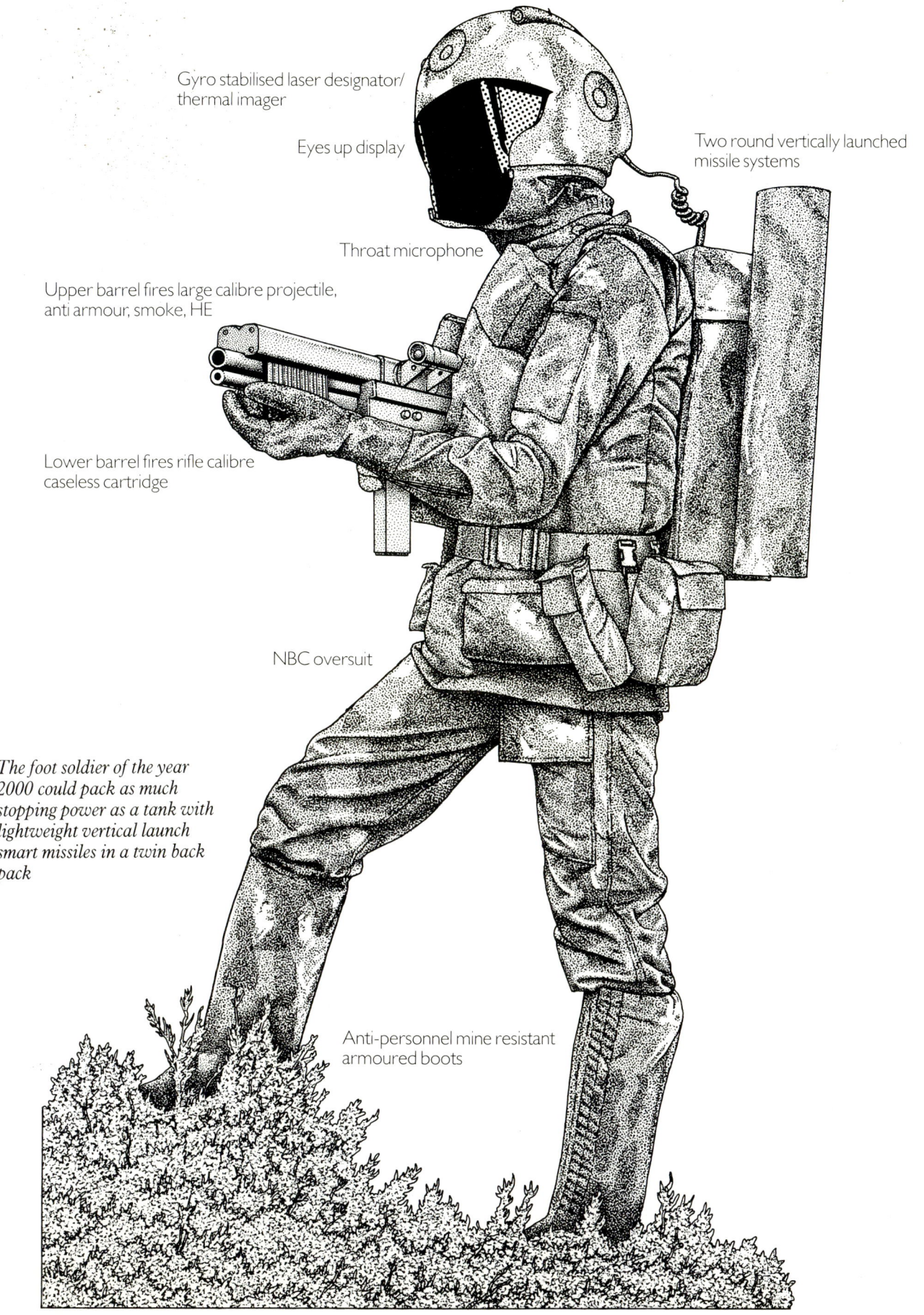

Gyro stabilised laser designator/
thermal imager

Eyes up display

Two round vertically launched
missile systems

Throat microphone

Upper barrel fires large calibre projectile,
anti armour, smoke, HE

Lower barrel fires rifle calibre
caseless cartridge

NBC oversuit

*The foot soldier of the year
2000 could pack as much
stopping power as a tank with
lightweight vertical launch
smart missiles in a twin back
pack*

Anti-personnel mine resistant
armoured boots

Conclusion

The defence of the West against an implacable, expansionist and militarised foe is an awesome responsibility. NATO remains (for the most part) an alliance of free democracies who must confront a totalitarian system without sacrificing its own political freedoms and it must continually strive to make legitimate in the eyes of its own people the use of their talent and treasure in that process.

But military men are tasked with thinking the unthinkable and making it routine, of constantly preparing for the worst case which will happen not next year but the next minute. At the same time soldiers and weapons scientists, like the authors of the AirLand Battle 2000 study, are tasked with peering into the short and long term future to read, not just the intentions of any potential enemy, but what the Pandora's box of technology may offer up. In the jargon they are both 'threat-' and 'technology-driven'.

In the age of nuclear deterrence however the casting of those plans, and their testing in operational manoeuvres and alerts, takes on the element of ritual because they are designed to ensure their own futility. The idea of deterrence (and maintaining conventional forces is as much about deterring an attack as building intercontinental ballistic missiles) contains the para-dox that it has to be 'believable' to ensure it should never be put to the test.

AirLand Battle doctrine is not about launching a nuclear Blitzkrieg on Eastern Europe, it is the way the US Army plans to fight and win if attacked. That of course means making the enemy 'lose' and that, it is argued, is the surest deterrent of all. But AirLand Battle still invokes the use of nuclear and chemical weapons, if militarily expedient and politically sanctioned to do so.

Follow on Forces Attack definitely does not rattle any nukes or binary shells but it is still a sub-concept of operations within Flexible Response where SACEUR's Nuclear Operations Plan waits to bring down the fearsome firepower of nuclear artillery, battlefield missiles and theatre weapons should a conventional defence, however it should be 'enhanced', fail.

'Deep strike', however it should be expressed, is about deterrence, a victim of the old paradox that it looks like a recipe for invoking war. If that war should come then deterrence has failed. Thenceforth the prospect of limited use of battlefield nuclear weapons is beset by awesome dangers. Any process or initiative which strives to deter war from starting in the first place and does so without using weapons of mass destruction, is something for free peoples to embrace.

Sikorsky LHX concept

GLOSSARY

APC   Armoured Personnel Carrier

Bundeswehr   Army of the Federal German Republic

Carrier Shell   Artillery round carrying sub-munitions

CENTAG   Central Army Group (NATO)

Conventional   Weapons and means of warfare other than nuclear or chemical

Dual-Key   Political sanction and operational procedure for two-nation involvement in release of nuclear weapons

Echeloning   Soviet principle of staging armed forces in successive waves

EMP   Electro magnetic pulse

ET   Emerging technology – developments at the threshold of science and technology

FEBA   Forward Edge of the Battle Area

FLIR   Forward Looking Infra Red

FLOT   Front Line of Troops

FM 100-5, Operations   US Army's Field Manual

FOFA   Follow On Forces Attack

Forward defence   NATO doctrine of defending as far forward as possible, that is on the soil of Western Germany

Frontal Aviation   Soviet tactical air force

GLCM   Ground Launched Cruise Missile

IFV   Infantry fighting Vehicle

ITV   Improved TOW Vehicle

J-SAK   Joint Second Echelon Attack

J-SEAD   Joint Suppression of Air Defences

JSTARS   Joint Stand Off Airborne Radar System

JTACMS   Joint Tactical Missile System

Kevlar   Very strong composite material

LHX   Light Helicopter Experimental programme

LTDP   Long Term Defence Procurement Programme

MBA   Main Battle Area

MBT   Main Battle Tank

MLRS   Multiple Launch Rocket System

Motor Rifle Division   Soviet mechanised infantry division

NATO   North Atlantic Treaty Organisation

NBC   Nuclear, Biological, Chemical

NOP   Nuclear Operations Plan

NORTHAG   Northern Army Group (NATO)

NSC   US National Security Council

OMG   Soviet Operational Manoeuvre Group

POMCUS   Prepositioning of Material Configured to Unit Sets (Equipment forward based in Europe awaiting reinforcing manpower)

REMBASS   Remote Monitored Battlefield Sensor System

RPV   Remotely Piloted Vehicle

SAC   Strategic Air Command (USAF)

SACEUR   Supreme Allied Commander Europe

SADM   Special Atomic Demolition Munition

SHAPE   Supreme Headquarters Allied Powers Europe

SIOP   Single Integrated Operations Plan (US strategic war plan)

SS   Surface to surface (missile)

Tactical nuclear weapon   Nuclear weapon configured for use on the battlefield against rival armed forces

Theatre weapons   Nuclear weapons configured for use over European ranges such as Britain – western Soviet Union

TNF   Theatre Nuclear Forces

TOW   Tube launched, Optically tracked, Wire guided – standard US heavy anti-tank missile

Tube Artillery   Support firepower based on traditional guns rather than rockets

USAFE   United States Air Forces Europe

USAREUR   US Army Europe

VISTA   Very Intelligent Surveillance and Target Acquisition

The publishers and the Research House would like to thank those individuals in the services, government departments, industry and the press who helped supply the illustrations for this book.

Front cover: Hughes Helicopter

titles: US Army (USA), 10–11: USA, 12: USA, 13: NATO, 15: USA, 16: USAF, 24–25: USA, 26–27: USAF, 28: USA, 29: Royal Artillery (UK MoD), 30–31: USA, 32: UKLF (MoD), 34: USA, 35: United Technologies, 36–37: Novosti, 39: Novosti, 41: USAF, 42: UKLF (MoD), 43: USAF, 44–45: USA, 46–47: COI, 48: USAF, 50–51: USA, 52: Swedish Army, 53: Hughes Aircraft, 54–55: USA, 56: USA, 58: NATO, 59: USA, 60: TRH, 61: USA, 62: USA, 64–65: USA, 66–67: USAF, 68: MBB, 69: Boeing, 70: USAF, 72: Austin Brown, 73: IAI, 74: USA, 76–77: USA, 79: Avco, 80: Martin Marietta, 81: Avco, 82–83: USAF, 84: Avco, 85: USAF, 86: Avco, Thompson-Brandt, 87: Emerson Electric, 88: Hughes Aircraft, 90: Martin Marietta, 91: Ford Aerospace, 92–93: Hughes Aircraft, 95: Bell Helicopter, 96–97: USA, 98: Honeywell, 99: USA, 100: USA, 101–102: USA, 104: Thorn-EMI, 105: Lockheed, 106: Thomson-CSF, 107: Norden, RCA, 108: Hughes Aircraft, 110–111: US DoD, 113: French Army, Hughes Aircraft, 114: *Bundeswehr*, 116: USA, *Bundeswehr*, 117: DoD, 120–121: Novosti, 122: Polish Army, 125: Novosti, 126–127: US DoD, 129: Novosti, 130: Novosti, 132: Novosti, 134–135: USA, 137: USA, 139: USA, 140–141: USA, 143: USA, 144: Emerson Electric, FMC Corporation, 147: Hughes Helicopter, 148: Emerson Electric, 150: 7USA, 152: USAF, McDonnell-Douglas, 153: USA, 154: Emerson Electric, USA, 157: USA, 158: USA, 159–170: USA, 172–173: USAF, 177: LTV, Bell, 178: Phalanx Corp, 179: Hughes Helicopter, 180: Scicon Ltd, 182: Sikorsky